Winning Blackjack
at Atlantic City
and Around the World

by Thor

A Citadel Press Book
Published by Carol Publishing Group

A Citadel Press Book
Published by Carol Publishing Group

Editorial Offices
600 Madison Avenue
New York, NY 10022

Sales & Distribution Offices
120 Enterprise Avenue
Secaucus, NJ 07094

In Canada: Musson Book Company
A division of General Publishing Co. Limited
Don Mills, Ontario

Manufactured in the United States of America

Library of Congress Cataloging-in-Publication Data

Gaffney, Thomas.
    Winning blackjack at Atlantic City and around the world / by
Thomas Gaffney.
        p.   cm.
    "A Citadel Press book."
    Includes bibliographical references.
    ISBN 0-8065-1178-8
    1. Blackjack (Game)   2. Gambling   3. Gambling—New Jersey—
Atlantic City.   I. Title.
GV1295.B55G34   1990
795.4'2—dc20   90-39521
                                                                  CIP

Carol Publishing Group books are available at special discounts
for bulk purchases, for sales promotions, fund raising, or
educational purposes. Special editions can also be created to
specifications. For details contact: Special Sales Department,
Carol Publishing Group, 120 Enterprise Ave., Secaucus, NJ 07094

Contents

To my wife, Jean

Foreword

The following conversation takes place between the late George Apley and his wife, Catherine, in the comfort of their sitting room on Boston's Beacon Street. The year is 1912.

CATHERINE
Is that why you didn't come to bed until two in the morning, George?

APLEY
Well, frankly, yes. It's really... quite interesting, if you face it tolerantly. It advances a theory that frankly never occurred to me.

CATHERINE
What's it about?

APLEY
Why—it's about the mind, really. The mind and the way human relationships affect the mind.

CATHERINE
What sort of relationships?

APLEY
Well—I don't know exactly how to put it, Catherine.

CATHERINE
Please say what you mean, George.

APLEY

Then I shall have to resort to a word that I have never used in your presence. It seems to be very largely a book about—sex.

CATHERINE

Oh! But how can he write a whole book about—that?

APLEY

Dr. Freud does seem to pad it a little, here and there.

Today, the question may be asked: How can you write a whole book about—blackjack, without seeming to pad it a little, here and there? You can if you assume that blackjack is just as intricate a diversion as say—that. Many books have been written about the game of blackjack covering its strategies, systems and rules. One area, however, still remains practically untapped. That is the game of blackjack as it is played in Atlantic City.

This book is written especially for the player at Atlantic City but also includes many other areas. No new strategies or systems are introduced. There are already enough counting systems to confuse the average player. So, if you know or use a counting system stick with it. If you do not, a simple high-low, one level system is used throughout this book.

If you are a successful basic strategy player and card counter this guide is not for you. You have done your homework and may spend your time more profitably playing in the casinos. *Winning Blackjack at Atlantic City and Around the World* is written exclusively for the beginner or intermediate player who would like to learn the game or improve his skills at the blackjack tables.

So read on. Learn and profit. And good winnings!

CHAPTER 1

How the Game Is Played

Blackjack is unique. A paradox. It is the simplest of card games and the most complex of card games. While the rules can be grasped in several minutes, few ever learn to play the game with any degree of proficiency.

Bridge is difficult. There are few really good bridge players despite the countless newspaper columns and scores of books written to help the player improve his game. Not to mention the ever-popular ten-session bridge courses that help to keep the YMCA's and YMHA's afloat. Pinochle, too, is a difficult game although no one writes about it. Perhaps it's just as well.

Then there are the card games, Old Maid and fish, for example, that are so simple that they appeal mostly to children. Consenting adults will play these infantile games only in the privacy of their homes. In a way, blackjack is that kind of a game. What could be simpler than a game decided by whichever side comes closer to a total of 21?

Yet many books have been written on how the game should be played and many blackjack schools charge their students Ivy League fees. Blackjack is the only casino game that is a headline maker. Have the craps tables and roulette wheels produced a Ken Uston? And from what other games have players been barred from the casinos for playing too well?

Reading the rules of a game can be pretty dry stuff, like witnessing the reading of a will. But important. First of all, it must be understood that blackjack is a contest between two

1

people: player and dealer. So when you take your place at a table, forget there are other players present. They are super-fluous and should be ignored.

The player in order to win must come closer to a point value of 21 than the dealer. Each playing card has the numeri-cal value assigned to it while all face cards count 10. With aces you have a choice. Count either 1 or 11, whichever makes you happy. If the player exceeds the magic number of 21, he immediately loses even though the dealer may do the same. And that is why the house has the edge. The player has the option of drawing (a hit) as many cards as he wishes to arrive at a total approaching 21. Or he may stand pat and not draw any cards if he thinks his two cards will beat the dealer. The dealer doesn't have this option. At Atlantic City, the dealer must draw to 16 and stand on 17.

In addition to hitting and standing, there are two other op-tions that a player may exercise. One is doubling-down in which the player elects to draw one more card and at the same time double his bet. An example: you are dealt a 7 and a 4 for a total of 11. The dealer's up-card is a 5, a weak card since he must take a hit to reach a total of at least 17. Since you believe your chance to beat the dealer is good, you dou-ble your bet.

The other option may be exercised when you receive a pair, any pair. You are permitted to split these two cards so you are, in effect, playing two separate hands. If you have a pair of 9's, for example, and the dealer shows a lowly 6, you may split your pair and very likely come up with two excellent hands. A king, queen, and jack are 10-value cards and considered a pair.

You are also permitted to combine splitting and doubling-down. For example, you are dealt a pair of 7's. You split the 7's and draw a 4 on the first 7 for a total of 11. You are allowed to double-down on the 11. However, you may not re-split. If you split a pair of 7's and receive a third 7, you cannot split this 7.

Just for the hell of it, let's run through a round with four players, each exercising one of the four options. Before any cards are dealt, the player must place his bet in the betting circle. Once the bet has been placed, *never* touch the chips. And if you are betting more than one denomination of chips, say a $1 chip and a $5 chip, place the $1 chip over the $5 chip. The lesser denomination chip always goes on top.

When all bets are placed, the game begins. The cards are dealt from the dealer's left to right, two cards face-up to each player; the dealer takes one card face-up, the other face-down. Now is decision-making time and the player's decision is based upon two variables: The total value of his two cards, and the value of the dealer's up-card. If the dealer's up-card is a high one, it should be assumed he has a strong hand. If a 10 or an ace is showing, he may have a blackjack . . . an ace with any 10-value card. This is the ultimate hand, the name of the game. If the player receives a blackjack, he is paid $3 for $2 wagered, unless the dealer also has a blackjack. In this case, the hand results in a tie (called a push in casino lingo) and no money is exchanged.

If the dealer's up-card is a low one, he has a potentially weak hand since he must draw at least one card with the possibility of drawing cards exceeding a total of 21 (called busting or breaking). For our example, let's give the dealer a 4.

Now that the deal is completed, the dealer points to the cards belonging to Player #1 at his left, called the first baseman, and announces the total value of his cards, "7." He has a 4 and a 3. Player #1 taps the table for a hit. *Never* say "hit" or "stand." Hand signals must be used. The hand signal for hit is a tap on the table or a come-forward motion signaling for an additional card. The dealer slides the next card out of the shoe for Player #1. It's a queen, giving him a total of 17. Player #1 waves his hand over the cards indicating stand.

The dealer then points to Player #2 saying, "11," since the player has a 7 and a 4. See, you don't even have to count. This is a lazy man's game. Player #2 replies "double-down" and moves out another bet equal in amount to his original one. The chips are placed just outside the betting circle since the original bet must never be touched. The dealer draws another card from the shoe and places it at right angles to the 7 and 4. It's a 9, giving Player #2 a total of 20. When you double-down you are entitled to receive only one additional card.

On to Player #3, who has a total of 19. Player #3 wisely decides to stand and indicates his decision by waving a hand palm-down over his cards.

Player #4 has a pair of 7's and tells the dealer to split. The dealer separates the cards, so now the player has two hands. Never, *never* touch the cards or the dealer will embarrass you for your gaucheness. Now each of the two hands is played separately. Player #4 receives a king on the first 7 and stands; a 9 on the second 7 and again stands. In splitting pairs you may draw as many cards as you wish except when splitting aces. Then you are entitled to only one card per ace.

The four players have made their decisions so the dealer flips over the hole card (down-card) with his up-card. It's a jack giving him a total of 14. As mentioned earlier, while the player has a decision to make, the dealer does not. He must draw to a 16 and stand on 17 even if he knows he has the players beaten. This rule is inflexible, so his play is never governed by the players' hands. The dealer draws his third card from the shoe...a 3. The dealer now has a total of 17 and must stand.

Pay out time. In paying out or raking in the chips (called checks by casino personnel), the dealer reverses direction. This time he works from his right to his left beginning with Player #4, who is called (what else?) the third baseman.

Player #4, remember, split a pair of 7's, so he was playing two hands, one totaling 16, the other 17. So the dealer rakes in the chips on the 16 and signals a tie by striking his wrist on the table announcing, "push" for the 17 and leaves the chips untouched.

Player #3 has a total of 19 and wins. The dealer places chips of equal value alongside the bet in the circle. Player #2 with a total of 20 is also paid. Player #1 with 17 is another push. No win, no loss.

That's all there is to it as far as the essentials of the game go. To summarize. The player has one of four decisions to make: hit, stand, double-down or split. Hit and stand are by far the most common decisions. Although Atlantic City rules permit a player to double-down on any two cards, there are only certain situations when it is wise to do so. Also, although any pair may be split, this move should be made only when it's to the player's advantage. Doubling-down and splitting pairs are basic strategy plays that will be treated later.

CHAPTER 2

Casino Environment

Those of you who have never visited a casino may find your first trip a bit unsettling. A casino is unlike any other place in the world. As you enter you will be struck immediately by the dark opulence, the glitz, the vitality, the nattily-attired dealers and the scantily attired cocktail waitresses. But most of all, by the hordes of people walking about aimlessly, reminding one of the toy departments of Macy's and Bamberger's two weeks before Christmas. But instead of carrying gifts, paper cups are carried containing coins for the slot machines. If you're a claustrophobiac, you may not survive. Casinos are windowless. The exit doors leading from the casinos do not open to the great outdoors. They open to a non-gaming area so that all contact with the outside world is completely shut off. And there are no clocks. Time in a casino has no meaning.

A few years ago, *Playboy* magazine ran an illustrated article featuring its newest casino, the seventh to open in Atlantic City. The photographs were very professional and pleasant to look at. But they were inaccurate. No one over the age of twenty-one was seen playing at the tables. No one was ugly. Or fat. Or poorly dressed. And everyone was smiling. Smiling! Fact: The typical facial expression worn by a player is *not* a smile. If they had included in their selected coverage, a fat little old lady toting a tacky paper cup, only then would the reader have a true picture of the way the inside of a casino *really* looks. A slight exaggeration, perhaps, but closer to the truth.

The first-time visitor is usually totally unprepared to see the vast sums of money being handled as if it weren't the real thing. Like funny money. Just the sight of $50 and $100 bills being tossed on the tables with complete abandon often causes first-arrivals to cringe or break out in goose bumps. Have no fear! In time, your sensitive feelings will be dulled. With a little practice, you will learn to cope and become as crass as the fellow playing next to you.

So much for the overall casino environment. Let's hike over to the blackjack area since it is here where you'll spend your happy hours. The blackjack table, your battlefield, is usually covered with green felt. To be different, Bally's Grand likes red while the Claridge prefers blue. Inscribed on the felt are the betting circles and a couple of inscriptions to make the player feel good. The key word is "Pays." "Insurance Pays 2 to 1" and "Blackjack Pays 3 to 2." This is casino psychology at its best.

We know that blackjack pays 3 to 2, but what about insurance? Anything that pays 2 to 1 certainly sounds good. Well, it is for the casinos. The way it works is that anytime the dealer gives himself an ace, the player can wager one-half his original bet that the dealer has a blackjack. If the dealer does have a blackjack, the player is paid 2 to 1. The trouble is, the odds are greater than 2 to 1 in favor of the casino. So just forget that the insurance option exists unless you are an expert card counter. Then there are times when you may wish to exercise this option.

Every blackjack table has a rectangular colored card or sign giving the minimum and maximum betting range for that table. At this stage of our development, we are not concerned with the maximum bet. Also, it spells out the rules for doubling-down and splitting. If you are searching (that's the proper word) for a $3 minimum table, it is, in most cases, not necessary to examine every sign, since the color of the sign usually indicates the minimum bet. A $3 minimum table will display a white sign which corresponds to a $1 white chip. A

$5 minimum table will have a red sign since a red chip is worth $5. A $10 minimum table uses a gold sign, and at a $25 minimum table you will find a green sign to correspond with the $25 green chip. Some casinos don't subscribe to color coding. They prefer gold no matter what the minimum is.

If you are successful in finding an unoccupied spot at a $3 table, temper your joy for the minimum may soon be raised at the discretion of the management. The floor person must give a half-hour notice to the table of the increase, but if you are not present when this notice is given, how are you to know? Well, sometimes the dealer will tell you, but don't count on it. When the floor person makes the announcement, he places the new minimum sign vertically behind the sign in use. So, if you're looking for a $3 table and see a red sign protruding behind the white...keep walking.

The floor person. What *is* his job? In the roped-off area behind the tables any number of people can be seen milling about meditatively, drinking coffee, or just puffing on a cigarette. We know they are casino employees since they wear ID badges complete with photos hanging from the lapels of their well-cut jackets. The lower the number they wear, the higher their rank.

But who are these people and why are they there? The most important person in this group is the pit boss. He is in charge of a section of tables, a pit. His primary function is to watch the floor persons working under him. The floor person's primary job is to watch the dealers assigned to him. Usually, there is one floor person assigned to two or three tables. So, everyone is watching everyone else. And they are all watching *you*...the player. To complete this picture, there is someone else watching from above. No, not God! They are security people in the gallery watching all the action through a one-way mirror called the "eye-in-the-sky."

If you are getting the impression that casinos have little faith in the innate honesty of man, especially their own employees, you are absolutely right. The dealer can make no move on his own. He must have a witness (the floor person) to his every act. He cannot shuffle, accept wager money, or change the chip denomination without calling upon the floor person to witness his action. And just a side note. Whenever you buy chips to enter a game, do not hand your money to the dealer. Place your bills in the betting area of the table. The dealer will then pick up your bills, examine both sides to make sure they are the real thing, and deposit them in a slot called "the drop." Whenever the dealer is relieved at the table, he must extend his arms upward to the "eye-in-the-sky" and spread his fingers to show that he's not pilfering a chip or two. Dealers have been known to hide chips in their hair (usually females), their mouth and any other part of their anatomy suitable for concealing chips. There is a story about a dealer who concealed a chip in his mouth. When he coughed, the chip went sailing through the air. He is no longer a dealer.

There are two accessories on the blackjack table. One is the shoe, a plastic box chained to the table that contains the cards to be dealt. It is called a shoe because it is shaped like ...you guessed it...a shoe box. The other accessory is called the discard tray, a plastic container (plastic is big in the casinos) for the cards that have been played. A player can easily tell by a glance at the discard tray how far the shoe has progressed. This information is important to the card counter, but of little value to anyone else.

There is one other accessory—this one attached unobtrusively to the back of the table. It, too, is plastic. It's called a toke box. A toke is a tip, so all tips given to the dealer are deposited by him in this box. Again, when the dealer receives a tip, he must tap the box with the chip to call it to the attention of the floor person. If a player wishes to tip the dealer (I never saw a dealer tip a player), he places the chip just outside the betting circle along with his regular bet.

CHAPTER 3

Basic Strategy

The world was an easier place in which to live twenty-five years ago. Then computer-aged technology changed this simple way of life. Instead of doing business with humans, we found ourselves dealing with intricate machines that were programmed to feed us with all the information we needed. And much that was not.

The computer revolutionized business. Information that formerly required hours of tedious work could now be obtained with accuracy within minutes, even seconds. Like all modern inventions that fall under the general heading of progress, the advent of the computer age brought mixed blessings.

One such blessing was the revolution in playing the game of blackjack. Until the early 1960s, blackjack was simply a game of luck or chance. Playing decisions were made solely on hunches. No thought was ever given to the laws of probability.

This approach was changed quite dramatically by Edward O. Thorp, a mathematics professor at the University of California. Professor Thorp's major fields of interest, not surprisingly, were probability and game theory. Game theory, incidentally, is far from new. It can be traced back to the 16th century and Geronimo Cardano, an Italian mathematician with a symbolic name.

Anyway, some twenty-five years ago when Professor Thorp announced his plans to spend his Christmas vacation in Las

10

Vegas, a colleague called his attention to an obscure article on blackjack strategy buried in a mathematical journal written several years earlier by a group of four mathematicians. Whereupon, Thorp looked up the article, summarized it, and made some crib notes.

He played in Vegas with pony in hand causing quite a stir. And, as they say, the rest is history. Professor Thorp, elated with his success at the gaming tables, returned home and studied The Game. He felt it could be beaten with the proper strategy. With the aid of an IBM 704 computer, he formulated a strategy even more effective than the one he used on his vacation. This strategy was published in 1962 in a book entitled *Beat the Dealer*, which immediately became a bestseller.

The casinos in Vegas were so nervous about the impact of this book that they hurriedly took countermeasures to protect their blackjack profits. They changed the rules. Doubling-down was no longer permitted except on 11, and they prohibited the splitting of aces. As a result, business at the blackjack tables dwindled considerably, and the casinos, realizing they overreacted, reinstalled the old rules. It took them only two weeks to do so.

But the casinos resorted to other measures to outwit the player. They shuffled a lot, especially when the player was winning. But they soon realized that this tactic proved costly to the house since it slowed up play. So they abandoned this strategy and introduced the two and four deck games. The battle between the casinos and the informed blackjack players was on and continues to this day.

To play blackjack with any degree of success at Atlantic City, it is essential to learn basic strategy. A great deal of time and energy have gone into tailoring the strategy to whatever rules are currently in use. Over nine billion computerized hands have been studied to refine this decision-making. When a decision was a marginal one, whether or not to split a pair of 4's against a dealer's 6, for example, three million hands were played before a basic strategy decision was finally made. With little time and effort, today's player can benefit enormously from this vast body of research. If he wishes to test the effectiveness of basic strategy, he can do what Professor Thorp did at Vegas many years ago—bring a pony. The dealers or pit bosses won't object if you keep it in your hand. But they probably won't permit you to lay it on the table.

But before going on to basic strategy according to the gospel of Atlantic City, let's take a little quiz designed to see how well *you* play the game. Circle the correct choice.

H = Hit   S = Stand   D = Double down   P = Split pair.

	YOUR HAND	DEALER UP-CARD	DECISION
1.	10,2	3	(H) S D P
2.	6,6	6	H S D (P)
3.	A,2	5	H S (D) P
4.	7,7	7	H S D (P)
5.	10,6	10	(H) S D P
6.	A,7	8	(H) (S) D P
7.	2,2	7	H S D (P)
8.	9,6	10	(H) S D P
9.	A,4	5	H S (D) P
10.	3,3	7	H S D (P)
11.	7,2	6	H S (D) P
12.	9,9	7	H (S) D P
13.	A,6	5	H S (D) P
14.	8,8	10	H S D (P)
15.	9,9	6	H S D (P)
16.	5,5	9	H S (D) P
17.	A,A	9	H S D (P)
18.	A,3	6	H S (D) P
19.	4,4	5	(H) S D P
20.	10,10	7	H (S) D P
21.	9,4	6	H (S) D P
22.	A,5	6	H S (D) P
23.	10,2	4	H (S) D P
24.	9,5	5	H (S) D P
25.	A,7	6	H S (D) P

The answers will be found at the end of this chapter.

This quiz is not an easy one because the hands are weighted heavily with pairs and aces, the most difficult hands to play correctly. Nevertheless, they are important hands because when you split and double-down, you have a double and sometimes triple bet.

One nice thing about Atlantic City basic strategy is uniformity. Your blackjack playing cousins in Nevada are not blessed with this advantage. There are Vegas rules and Northern Nevada rules. Since every casino in Vegas makes up its own rules, the basic strategy player can become easily confused. He has to learn downtown Vegas single deck, downtown Vegas multiple deck, Vegas Strip single deck, and Vegas Strip multiple deck. In Northern Nevada, too, he is confronted with single and multiple deck games with many rule variations.

Anyway, here are the basic strategy rules to follow in Atlantic City. The first group does not include player's hands showing aces or pairs. These two groups follow.

PLAYER'S HAND	PLAYER'S DECISION ON DEALER'S UP-CARD
9	Double on 3 to 6. Otherwise hit
10	Double on 2 to 9. Hit on 10,A
11	Double on 2 to 10. Hit on A
12	Stand on 4 to 6. Otherwise hit
13 to 16	Stand on 2 to 6. Otherwise hit
17 to 21	Always stand

PLAYER'S HAND WITH ACES	
A,2 & A,3	Double on 5 and 6. Otherwise hit
A,4 & A,5	Double on 4 through 6. Otherwise hit
A,6	Double on 3 through 6. Otherwise hit
A,7	Double on 3 through 6. Stand on 2, 7 and 8. Hit on 9, 10, A
A,8 to A,10	Always stand
A,A	Always split

**PLAYER'S
PAIRS**

2,2 & 3,3	Split on 2 through 7. Otherwise hit
4,4	Split on 5 and 6. Otherwise hit
5,5	Never split. Treat as a 10
6,6	Split on 2 through 6. Otherwise hit
7,7	Split on 2 through 7. Otherwise hit
8,8	Always split
9,9	Split on 2 through 9 except 7. Stand on 7, 10 and A
10,10	Always stand

All the above decisions assume that the player holds two cards. If the player holds 3, 4 or 5 cards (a multi-card hand), the same basic strategy is used.

IF THE DEALER HAS:	**HIT UNTIL YOU HAVE:**
2 or 3	13
4, 5 or 6	12
7 or higher	17 (hard)

For an example of a multi-card hand, suppose your first two cards total 5. You take a hit and receive a 4 for a total of 9. Another hit and you draw a 3 for a total of 12. If the dealer has a 4, 5 or 6, you stand. If the dealer has a 2 or a 3 up-card, you would take a hit since you are shooting for 13. One more example: You again receive a total of 5 for your first two cards. Taking a hit you draw a queen for a total of 15. The dealer shows an 8. The table tells us if the dealer has a 7 or higher card showing, hit until you have at least 17, so in this case you take a hit.

If you are reading this chapter with undivided attention, you will notice that in a multi-card hand, the instructions are if a dealer has a 7 or higher, you hit until you have a *hard* 17 as opposed to a *soft* 17. Getting complicated, eh? A soft hand is any hand in which the ace can be counted as either 1 or 11. An ace, 6 for example, may be counted as 7 or 17, a soft hand. However, if your hand consists of an ace, 6 and 5 the ace can only count as 1 for a total of 12, a hard hand. Counting the ace as 11 would, of course, give a total of 22 and break. Simply put, a soft hand has two possible totals. Who ever said this game was simple? In addition, *always* hit soft 14 through soft 17 in an attempt to improve your hand. A soft 18 is not as powerful as most players think it is. So the strategy with a soft 18 is to stand if the dealer's up-card is 8 or less; if 8 or more, take a hit. Always stand on soft 19 through 21. You'll have a hell of a time improving such a hand.

That's about all there is to basic strategy. Memorize the tables and practice with a deck of cards. It is estimated that most players can learn these tables in two hours. So try it, and see if you pass this test. After you learn the basic strategy well enough so it becomes second nature, practice for a few minutes several times a week. Repetition is important. The night before you plan to visit a casino, extend your practice session about a half hour or so. It will pay dividends.

In addition, practice your basic strategy with flash cards. It is easy to make up a handwritten set. Just take a sheet of unlined white paper and outline squares about 2 inches by 2 inches. Print in large numbers various hands that will be dealt to you. For example 6,6; A,A; 11; 16; A,7. About 24 combinations will do. Then glue the squares to any stiff paper. Cut them out and put the answer on the reverse side. For example, you have a flash card showing 2,2 on the front, turn the card over and it will read, "Split on 2 - 7. Otherwise hit." These cards are easy to carry in your pocket or purse and you can run through them in a matter of seconds. Once again, practice until you are able to flip through the cards with no hesitation.

And now for the answers to the quiz.

1. H	6. S	11. D	16. D	21. S
2. P	7. P	12. S	17. P	22. D
3. D	8. H	13. D	18. D	23. S
4. P	9. D	14. P	19. P	24. S
5. H	10. P	15. P	20. S	25. D

Score 4 points for each correct answer.

SCORE RATING

96–100 Congratulations! You know your basic strategy and are ready to count cards. You made the Dean's list.

84–92 You play an above-average game and have a respectable record at the blackjack tables. A little work with your flash cards will make you a winner.

72–80 You are a member of the great unwashed. An average player without much success at the blackjack tables. Maybe a winning session now and then.

68–0 Shame on you! Don Rickles would say, "Dummy!" The casinos love you and hope you continue your losing ways.

To summarize: There is only *one* basic strategy for Atlantic City blackjack. This strategy must be learned and understood until it becomes second nature. Card drills and flash cards are your aids to learning basic strategy. Practice regularly.

CHAPTER 4

Profile of the Typical Blackjack Player

Now that we know all there is to know about basic strategy, let's take a breather before tackling the main course, card counting, and reflect on the level of play of the typical Atlantic City blackjack player who is, in a word, a masochist. The quality of play at our favorite gaming mecca is strictly bush league. And this indictment is as true of the quarter ($25) bettor as it is of the $3 bettor. The typical Atlantic City blackjack player has a death wish.

Blackjack is a game of skill offering the best odds to the player of any casino game. But this is true only if his play is skillful. The hunch player is often no better off than the slot machine player who on the average, contributes to the house fifteen cents out of every dollar deposited in the little monster.

Unfortunately, the typical blackjack player at Atlantic City is a hunch player who hasn't the foggiest idea of how to place a bet. And he is guided by a plethora of gambling superstitions completely alien to the knowledgeable blackjack player. Luck, he thinks, is the only ingredient that will make him a winner. He believes, for example, the way the cut card is placed is important. And if the last shoe was kind to him, he urges the same player who inserted the cut card to place it again. The third baseman (the last position dealt) is carefully watched and coached since his decision determines the card the dealer will draw if he has less than 17.

Just for the hell of it, let's observe a typical blackjack player on a visit to his favorite Atlantic City casino. Let's try to enter into his thought processes and see what it takes to make a loser.

After a tiring two-hour drive, our victim arrives early on a Saturday afternoon. He is starving and forty-fifth in the waiting line for a meal at the casino deli. Almost two hours later and $12.95 poorer, he heads for the blackjack area. By now the tables are crowded. Ah, there's a spot! He squeezes (the seats are not designed for big people) into a seat at the far end of the table to the dealer's right. He is the third baseman whether or not he realizes it. After plunking down a crisp new $50 for chips, he is dealt a 15 while the dealer draws a queen. After much deliberation he announces, "I'll stand." "You'll have to use hand signals, sir," says the dealer in a condescending way. Slightly embarrassed, he waves his hand over his cards. The dealer flips over her downcard with the queen . . . it's a 6. She draws another card from the shoe . . . a 5 for a total of 21 and gathers up the players chips.

The first card out of the shoe in the next round is a king. "See that! You should have taken a hit," growls the first baseman. "The dealer would have busted!"

"What are you, an expert?" shoots back the third baseman.

Just then, a cocktail waitress appears by the table. "Scotch on the rocks," orders our man at third. He urgently feels the need for one.

In baseball parlance, the third base position is called the "hot spot." It's also the "hot spot" at the blackjack table since the third baseman's decision to stand or hit determines the dealer's next card if he is required to draw. So a questionable decision by the third baseman may alienate him from his fellow players. He can become a pariah in less time than it takes to play a shoe. So, if you don't know basic strategy, avoid the "hot spot." To go a step further, avoid the game completely until you know it.

In less than a half hour, our third baseman's chips are reduced to two reds. He withdraws another $50 bill from his money clip. His hope of returning home a winner is now slightly diminished. He decides to employ a betting strategy: if he loses a round, he will double his bet and keep doubling until he wins. Four rounds later his chips have vanished. "The gods," he murmurs, "are not smiling on me today." He takes a swig of his Scotch. "Nonsense!" he concludes, "that's not the reason at all. Everyone at this table is losing. It's the dealer! The dealer just happens to be 'hot' and there's only one way to cope with a 'hot' dealer — find yourself another table."

After a 20-minute search our Typical Player finds a vacant seat at another table. This time he is the first baseman occupying the first seat at the dealer's left. No longer will he have to listen to the criticism of the fools he had been playing with. They were destroying his self-confidence and affecting his game. Without self-confidence, he reasons, he will not be a winner. Now he can relax and play a really solid game.

Taking two $50 bills from his money clip he orders chips and another Scotch on the rocks. He bets one red chip and wins. "Hell!" he mutters, "I should have bet two." He pushes out two red chips confidently and leans back in his seat.

"Thirteen," the dealer says with a touch of annoyance in his voice. "Thirteen," as he gestures to the first baseman's cards. "Hit."

The dealer hits with a 10 for a total of 23 and bust. "Why the hell did I hit when the dealer has a lousy 4 showing?" he asks himself. "He hurried me, that's why. That's the worst part of playing first base. You don't have enough time to make a sound decision."

By the time the drink arrives, he has lost another $40. He is becoming angry with the dealer who, he thinks, is too fast and impatient. After all, he is here to relax and enjoy himself, not be pressured by some gung-ho dealer with his eye on a pit boss's job. And he knows he's getting more than his share of stiff hands. Almost every hand, it seems, calls for a tough decision.

Well, he can't control the cards the ill-mannered dealer is giving him, but he can alter his betting technique. It seems every time he bets three or four chips he loses; when he bets only one or two chips, he wins. Once when he tried to add another chip to his original bet because he suddenly felt lucky, the dealer became very upset. That's when the pit boss came over and whispered something to the dealer. It was unnerving. The palms of his hands are beginning to sweat.

While gulping his Scotch (usually he sips his favorite drink), he makes a decision: he's been playing too timidly, far too conservatively. The spoils belong to the brave; a wishy-washy bettor deserves to lose. So he begins to bet with greater abandon.

He drains his glass and orders another. He wins four consecutive rounds, and the fourth was a real winner. Splitting a pair of 10's against the dealer's 7, he draws an ace and a 9, winning both hands. His confidence restored, he now splits every pair and doubles-down every time the dealer shows a low card. There are periods when he feels he can't lose, and at one point is well on his way to recover his losses.

However, three Scotches later, and feeling slightly tipsy, his entire bankroll of $700 is gone. Ruin, as they say in the trade.

Enough of this. Let's leave the poor slob to his hangover. But this scene, with many variations on a theme by Lady Luck, is being enacted at every moment in every casino in Atlantic City. This little scenario is not an isolated case. The combination of no basic strategy, lack of money management, and too much booze is certain to result in a losing session for the gambler and a nice win for the casino. A casino wins between $2 million and $5 million every month from the typical blackjack player!

The moral of this little profile is to point out the need for learning how the game of blackjack should be played. When you take your place at the table facing the dealer, you are facing a professional. The dealer is well trained to do what he's supposed to do: make money for the casino. It is your job to see that he fails.

CHAPTER 5

Card Counting

You are now a blackjack player, of sorts. You know the mechanics of the game and basic strategy. If you put your newly acquired knowledge to work in a visit to your favorite Atlantic City casino, you will, no doubt, be amused by the dumb play of the other players sitting at your table. The player on your right, for example, splitting 10's, and the player on your left consistently standing on 14 and 15 against the dealer's ace or 10. And their indecisiveness! Not knowing whether to hit or stand, to split or not to split, and when to double-down. They stare at the shoe interminably trying to divine what the next card will be, then signal for a hit and bust. "The last three cards were high...a low card was due to come up," is the wisdom imparted on anyone willing to listen. Don't scorn them. You were in that league not too long ago.

But there is one more important hurdle to clear before you become a really proficient player. Playing perfect strategy, unfortunately, will no longer give you an edge over the house. Before the elimination of the early surrender rule in the spring of 1981, the basic strategy player had a slight edge (.2 percent), but now, sadly, the odds have shifted in favor of the casino. There is only one way, despite widely-advertised schemes to the contrary, to turn the odds to your favor—and that is to learn how to count cards.

And counting cards is not difficult. That's not to say it's easy; it requires concentration and practice. But it is not difficult. Whether or not you were good at math in school has no bearing on your ability to count cards. And there are the fringe benefits. A card counter, you will learn, gains respect. Rodney Dangerfield obviously is no card counter. When anyone discovers you are a blackjack player, the inevitable question is asked: "Are you a counter?" Unless the question comes from a casino employee, tell the truth. Immediately, you'll gain in stature since the layman views the card counter as a superman, magician and mystic.

Now for some examples to show why card counting works. First, remove all the 5's and 6's from a deck of cards. Play a number of practice hands and keep score to see how often you win. You will win about seventy percent of the time since 5's and 6's are the dealer's favorite cards. Now, withdraw all jacks and 10's and keep score. Your luck has deserted you; you are no longer a winner. The more aces and 10's in a deck, the greater the chances are of a player winning. The more low cards in a deck, the greater is the certainty that the player will lose.

If you toss a coin, playing heads and tails and four consecutive heads appear, heads will still have a fifty percent chance of coming up on the fifth toss since each toss is an independent event. The same is true of the roll of the dice and a spin of the roulette wheel. If seven consecutive reds appear, the chances of red coming up on the next roll are still the same. The only casino game that is not governed by the independent event law is blackjack. The cards remaining to be played in the shoe are determined by the cards that have already been played and stacked neatly at rest in the discard tray. This is why card counting works. Therefore, if a proportionately large percentage of high cards remain in the shoe, the odds favor the player. And the greater the percentage of high cards, the greater are the odds in favor of the player and the higher his bet should be. In the long run, a card counter is going to lose slightly more hands than he wins, but he compensates for this by using a betting range of at least 1 to 5, betting low when the odds are against him, and increasing his bet as the odds become more favorable. Does it really work? The casinos know it does.

There is an infinite variety of card counting systems ranging from a simple ace-five system to the highly sophisticated advance counting techniques used by professionals. The ace-five system works like this: The 5 is assigned a value of + 1; the ace is counted as –1. So, when the deck is plus, more 5's than aces have been played and the player's bet will increase. If the count is minus, more aces than 5's have been played and a minimum bet is wagered. The ace-five system is now practically obsolete and of little value in playing the Atlantic City 6-deck or 8-deck game. It can best be used as a supplement to a more effective system.

At the other extreme are the complex advance counting systems used by a small group of professionals. The techniques used have been highly refined and give the player the best advantage over the house. They are multi-level counts as opposed to the more widely-used one-level systems. In these systems, every card is assigned a plus or minus value. There are not many people, however, who have the time and are willing to devote the energy to learn a multi-level system.

A good workable card counting system is the high-low point count developed over twenty years ago by Harvey Dubner and refined over the years by Stanford Wong and Julian Braun. This system is very effective and easy to learn. A value of + 1 is assigned to low cards . . . 2, 3, 4, 5, and 6; a value of – 1 is given high cards . . . ace, king, queen, jack and 10; and no value is assigned to neutral cards . . . 7, 8 and 9. For example, the following cards are seen: 7, 4, Q, A, 9, J, 6 and 3. Your running count would be: 0 (7 is a neutral card); + 1 (4); 0 (the Q is a –1, so with a + 1 count and a –1, the running count equals 0); –1 (A); still –1 (9); –2 (J); –1 (6) and 0 (3). So, the count for these eight cards consisting of three plusses (4, 6 and 3); three minuses (Q, A and J) and two neutral cards (7 and 9) equals 0.

Here's an easy one. Give the running count for the following: 6, 2, 5, 3, 10, 4 and 2. With all these low cards you will immediately see that the count is strongly positive. Okay, let's count: +1, +2, +3, +4, +3 (10 is −1, so subtract 1 from the running count of 4), +4, +5. Easy?

Now for a more difficult count. Try counting, 10, J, A, 2, Q, K, 10. A glance will tell you that the count is strongly negative. The count is −1, −2, −3, −2 (2 is a +1, so with a running count of −3, a +1 = −2), −3, −4 and −5. There are six minus cards (10, J, A, Q, K and 10) and one plus card (2) for a running count of −5. When you are counting, by the way, don't think *minus* 5, think *M* 5. Since you will be counting with some degree of speed, it helps to shorten, even in your mind, the minus to a simple M. Beginner counters find it more difficult to work with a negative count than a positive count. Don't let this bother you.

Start counting as soon as you see the dealer's upcard. The dealer, remember, starts a round by dealing each player one card face-up. This is an excellent time to let your eyes rest on the attributes of a well-endowed cocktail waitress or handsome dealer. Or light a cigarette if you're still addicted. It is not card counting time yet. Then, zing! The dealer draws a card face-up, a 10. This is the first card you count. The first baseman receives his second card. You combine the value of his two cards into a single count. Say he is lucky enough to draw a blackjack. His ace counts −1 and his 10 counts −1, so first baseman's total is −2. Since you already counted the dealer's 10 as −1, the running count is now −3. Continue around the table counting each player's two cards as a single unit. A 10,7, for example, is counted as −1, a 10,3 = 0.

The toughest part of counting is keeping up with a fast dealer while dealing the second up-card to the table. The moment of truth. Practice this at home along with the other card drills described in the next chapter.

After the second card has been dealt to the third baseman, counting becomes a lot easier. Now, only one card at a time is drawn from the shoe, and due to the indecisiveness of the players, the pace slows considerably. Counting is now duck soup for any self-respecting counter.

There is not a living card counter who has not at one time lost the count—or dropped the count as they say in the trade. Well, at least it's not embarrassing since he is the only one who is aware of it. But, what to do? Well, there are a couple of options. If you are not sure, for example, whether the count is a +4 or +5, continue to play using the more conservative +4 count. If you completely lose the count, ask the dealer to hold your place and take a walk. The dealer will hold your spot at the table for about fifteen minutes. Then time your return for the beginning of a new shoe.

Ideally, you should not play at a table for more than forty-five minutes to an hour. The average person's attention span begins to falter after an hour or so. Take a walk along the boardwalk or go to another casino. Sometimes, too, you can take a break from counting without even leaving the table. Suppose the count is −14 (a horrible count) and approximately two rounds remain in the shoe. Why bother to count?

As a beginner card counter, you will now view the blackjack tables at the casinos with a different eye. Before learning to count, you didn't pay much attention to the dealer. Basically, they were all the same. It didn't matter if they were fast or slow, called out the count or not, or where they placed the cut card. But when you're a card counter, the dealer's style takes on added importance. Some dealers are very fast and use a lot of hand motions—and wear glistening rings adorning every finger. These dealers are to be avoided. As a beginner, make it easy for yourself. Find the slowest dealer you can. And there are enough of them. Since the turnover in this job is relatively high, it is always possible to find a novice dealer fresh from dealer school. Grab him!

Also, patronize a dealer who calls out the count loud and clear. Unless you're experienced, counting becomes difficult when you draw four or five low cards and try to add their total and count at the same time. Let the dealer count for you.

Also, look for a dealer who places the cut card far to the rear. The fewer number of cards behind the cut card, the more accurate your count will be.

As a beginner counter sharpen your skills at a low minimum table, which may be as difficult to find as a moderately priced meal in a casino. Sometimes, depending on the whim of the casino, a $3 table can be found for an hour or two shortly after opening, so try to arrange for a morning visit. The weekends are the worst times to play, especially during the warmer months of the year. The best month to play is December. Christmas shopping vies with the casinos for disposable income. You don't have to wait for December, of course, but it's nice to know that it's the ideal month in which to play.

Way back when you were a Typical Player, your position at the table made little or no difference. And why should it? But, as a card counter, especially a fledgling counter, where you sit *does* make a difference. The beginner counter should find a spot near the middle of the table, or better still, somewhere between the middle and the third baseman. It is difficult to see the cards from the first baseman's positions, particularly if you are over forty and wear bifocals. The first baseman occupies the poorest position since he must make his decision as soon as the cards are dealt. The beginner counter who has fallen a little behind in the count doesn't need this added pressure. It is more comfortable to be the fourth or fifth player and have ample time to look at the cards and catch up, if necessary, on the count. But, take note. You can't afford to fall behind in your count, at least not more than a split-second because if the first baseman takes a hit and breaks, his cards are scooped up by the dealer faster than you can say . . . well, whatever you wish to say.

One more tip for the beginner card counter—don't drink anything intoxicating while you play. No matter how well you think you can hold your liquor, drinking and counting do not mix. The only exception to this rule is to order a drink just before you plan to stop playing.

On your first visit to a casino after learning to count and practicing your card drills faithfully, do not immediately take your place at a table. First, look for a table where the dealer is shuffling and stand behind the players and practice counting. See how well you do. You could do a lot worse than back count, as the experts call it, your entire first session at the casino, especially if your confidence is shaky. Confidence will come in time. It takes about fifty hours of casino play to really feel at home. The casino environment, with a musical group playing in the background, the shouts of the craps players, and attractive young things in scanty attire hustling drinks, is not conducive to concentration. Professional football players sometime practice their plays in a hotel room with the television or radio volume at full blast to simulate the noise of the crowd on a Sunday afternoon. You can use this same technique while practicing your drills. Well, maybe not full blast, but you get the idea.

Let's summarize why card counting works. High cards favor the player; low cards favor the house. If by counting we know that a high percentage of 10's and aces remain in the shoe, we increase our bets since the odds are in our favor. If the count is negative, that is a high percentage of low cards remain in the shoe, we place minimum bets since the odds are against us. The two most important cards to a dealer are the 5 and 6 since he must hit a stiff hand (any hand totaling 12 through 16). In the long run the number of hands we win playing basic strategy will be slightly less than the number of hands we lose. The only way to compensate for this unfortunate fact is to count cards and increase our bets when the count is positive.

CHAPTER 6

Card Drills

Now for the bad news. It is not enough to know *how* to count cards. You must learn to count with speed and accuracy. And the place to do this is not at the casinos with your hard-earned money, but at home. Like playing the piano, the more you practice the better you become. As a famous concert pianist once remarked, "If I miss one day's practice. *I* know. If I miss two day's practice, the *audience* knows."

And practice at home can be fun—and a challenge. In blackjack drills, as in golf, you are competing against yourself. A suggested practice drill, excellent to increase your skills in both basic strategy and card counting is:

1. Run through your flash cards several times. They are the most important tool in your kit. And carry them with you at all times. You will be surprised how many times you can run through them in the course of a day. Have them handy while driving and riffle through them while waiting for the traffic light to change. So, let the driver behind you honk his horn in irritation. You're learning, he's not.

2. Deck scan. Hold a deck of cards face-up in one hand and move them as quickly as possible into the other hand counting by two's. With some practice you will scan a deck in 15-20 seconds. Time yourself and repeat this exercise four times.

3. Single-card countdown. Hold a deck of cards face-down in

one hand and flip each card over face-up with the other hand, counting as you go. When you can do this drill in 20-25 seconds you are ready for the big time. Repeat three times.

4. Two-card countdown. This drill is the same as the single-card countdown except two cards at a time are flipped over. Since this is the way you'll be counting much of the time, this drill is very valuable. With practice you should complete this drill in 20-25 seconds. Again, repeat three times.

5. Deal out 7 cards, then a second round of 7 cards, just as the dealer does in real life, starting your count with the first two-card pattern. For this drill, forget the dealer exists. So, you will be dealing three rounds of 14 cards and one round of 10 cards. Repeat this drill three times.

6. Deal a 3-hand game including the dealer. Use basic strategy for each of the three players while counting. In the same way, deal out a 4-hand plus dealer game, and finally a 5-hand plus dealer game. These are excellent drills for both basic strategy and counting.

7. Practice soft hands. Run through the deck using a constant player A,2. Turn the first card face-up; this is the dealer's up-card—a 5. So, the rule is double-down. Turn the next card face-up, which again will be the dealer's up-card—a king. Now you are shooting for a 17 or better. You hit your A,2, receiving another 2 for a total of 5 or 15. You hit again—a 10. Now you have a hard 15. Another hit is called for—a 7 for a total of 22 or bust. Too bad. The next card drawn will, of course, be the dealer's up-card. And so on through the deck. Another soft-hand to be practiced is A,7, which is the trickiest of all soft hands. The rule, remember, is double-down on 3 through 6; hit on 9, 10 and A; and stand on 2, 7 and 8. When you have mastered the

A,7 soft hand, you will have it made. All the other soft hands are simpler.

8. Now for the final drill. Here we use 6 decks, simulating the 6-deck Atlantic City shoe game. Shuffle the cards and deal a seven player and dealer game. When you come to the very last card, your count will be 0. It's not? You dropped the count, so play another 6-deck game. In fact, play another 6-deck game whether or not you lost the count. And keep trying to increase your speed. This is when your knowledge of basic strategy comes in handy. Know it instinctively. You will not have time to think about a playing decision and count at the same time. Basic strategy must become second nature to you. This drill is the greatest of them all since it is a simulation of the real thing.

In reading about these drills, they may appear to be very time-consuming. They are not. After a few weeks practice, you will be able to run through these eight drills in less than forty-five minutes, or less time than it takes to watch *General Hospital*. For the first month, you should run through these drills daily. The first two weeks will show marked improvement in accuracy and drill time. Then you will notice that your progress will slow up a bit until you reach a plateau at the end of the first month. At this point, you can confine your drills to every other day.

Now for a few additional thoughts about drill times. You know when you make errors in counting, but how do you know how well you are coming along with your speed? The suggested drill times already mentioned give the answer. These drill times are related to the average dealer, whatever that is. To compete with a fast dealer you should be able to scan a deck in sixteen seconds; go through a single-card countdown in twenty seconds and the two-card countdown in twenty seconds. For the first week or two, do not be discouraged if your times seem awfully slow. It it takes you two minutes to count down a deck of cards, so what?

The faster you count the easier it will be for you when you make your debut as a counter. On this historic day, you will probably drop the count on several shoes. That's to be expected. So, before taking your place at a table, prepare as an athlete would—warm up. Look for a dealer who is not an automaton and stand behind his table and practice counting a shoe or two. Time spent in this way is not wasted. By the end of your first session, you will know where your weaknesses lie. Make notes that may be helpful on future visits.

CHAPTER 7

The Female Blackjack Player

There are still places in the world, particularly clubs, bars and restaurants, where a lone woman is not welcome. If she is lucky enough to be seated at the restaurant of her choice, chances are the maître d' will escort her to a table in some obscure corner or halfway into the kitchen.

The Atlantic City casinos do not operate this way. They welcome women, alone or with friends. They are among the few places where a woman can travel anytime of the day or night and have a genuinely good time. And a safe one.

A lot of women know this and do not hesitate to hop a bus when things get boring at home or when they have a spat with their husbands or boyfriends. It beats buying a new hat. If a woman lives within a hundred or so miles of Atlantic City, there are countless buses heading for the casino mecca at all hours at extremely low fares. The buses are fast, clean and comfortable and chauffered by courteous drivers. The contempt with which bus travel is generally held does not apply to Atlantic City. You will find it a lot more fun to join the crowd than to sit alone in your living room watching the soaps.

Too many women, however, deprive themselves of a *really* good time, and a profitable time, by heading herd-like for the slot machines as soon as they pass through the casino doors. This practice is encouraged by the casinos which hand out

$10 in quarters to their bus patrons. Never do they hand out $10 in chips. And there is a reason for this. The slots are very profitable to the casino. Ladies, you don't stand a chance of beating the slots. They return eighty-five cents or less for every $1 deposited. And, let's admit it: playing the slots is boring—about as much fun as dropping coins in a vending machine for a newspaper or a pack of cigarettes.

The next time you visit a casino look for five-cent slot machines. And you will have to look hard because the casinos locate them in some obscure corner of the house, unlike the $1 slots which are visible everywhere. In front of a row of five-cent slots, you will find a group of uncomfortably seated females dropping nickel after nickel into these metal containers while pulling the handle. Another nickel, another pull of the handle. Hour after hour, these glassy-eyed ladies continue their ritual hoping to fill their cardboard containers. An exercise in futility. To be perfectly frank and impartial, you will find an occasional male in this setting. But, essentially, this is a female world. There is absolutely no thought or skill attached to this pastime. It is the lowest form of gambling.

So why are the slots so popular? Perhaps because there are no rules to learn, no decisions to be made, no possibilities of dumb plays, and no thought or concentration required. But also, no money to be made; the more you play, the more you lose. Really, ladies, this is the pits.

You will find a lot of women at the blackjack tables. Not nearly though as many as there should be. And their standard of play is about the same as the men's, which is not saying a hell of a lot. But there are differences in style. I've seen any number of women use a basic strategy crib card or pony; it is rare to see a man use one. Men won't admit they don't know how to play the game. Just because they played some blackjack in their service days, they think they know the game. And women have less self-confidence than men. How many times have I seen a woman turn to her escort and ask, "Do I hit or stand, Arnold?" She shouldn't ask because Arnold doesn't know, but it won't stop him from giving an incorrect answer. I've yet to see a man ask a woman for advice on blackjack.

This may sound obvious, a truism perhaps, but there are only two reasons why anyone would want to go to a casino: to enjoy the games and to win. The more you know about the game, the greater your enjoyment will be and the better your chances of returning home a winner. Learn basic strategy before you risk your money at the tables, or *you* will pay as you learn. Even though you haven't mastered card counting, a knowledge of basic strategy will enable you to play a better game than over ninety percent of your fellow players. And you will never experience an indecisive moment. Your decisions will be sound, based upon millions of computerized hands. The place to practice your strategy is *not* in the casino, however. It is too costly. Practice at home. When you feel comfortable with it, climb behind the wheel of your car or hop a bus. In the long run, you will probably lose a little money since the odds are slightly in favor of the house. But, the odds for the blackjack player using basic strategy are far better than any other casino game, and certainly far better than the slots.

The next logical step is to learn card counting and swing the odds in *your* favor. Once you have mastered basic strategy, counting is not difficult. But without a knowledge of basic strategy, card counting is impossible. Buy six decks of cards and practice the card drills described in this book. Try to set aside a definite time for practice. When you find yourself improving in accuracy and speed, you will really enjoy these sessions.

Women love a bargain. It is part of the female psyche to shop where the dollar buys the best value. Apply this concept on your trips to the casinos, and do not waste your time and money on games that separate you from your bankroll. Head for the bargain table. It is the smart thing to do.

CHAPTER 8

Money Management

The single most important item in becoming a winning blackjack player is often the most neglected—money management. Paradoxically, it is the easiest facet of the game to learn, but the most difficult to adhere to. Simply put, money management consists of a set of guidelines that suggests how much to bet in a variety of situations.

The typical gambler has no use for money management. It cramps his style. Caught up in the excitement of the game, he bets with an abandon certain to cause his downfall. Assuming that he plays solid basic strategy and counts with some degree of skill, without money management he will lose in the long run. It is inevitable since money management is sixty-five percent of the game.

Just as in investing, the preservation of a player's capital tops the list in any set of monetary objectives. So, the purpose of money management is to remain solvent while maximizing favorable situations. An old stock market adage says, "Buy at wholesale, sell at retail." For our purpose, we could amend that a little and say, "Bet minimum when negative, maximum when positive."

It is seldom easy to find agreement among experts in any field since experts are, by definition, prima donnas. There is agreement however among the giants on the blackjack scene on the followings three points:

1) A casino bankroll must be set aside for playing purposes

only. This fund is untouchable, and not to be used for any other cause, no matter how worthy.

2) The minimum bankroll should be $300. If you can't raise this rather insignificant amount of money, you have no business at the blackjack tables.

3) Keep an accurate record of your casino visits (no matter how painful at first). List which casinos you play in, your wins and losses, and the number of hours spent playing.

Now for the betting strategy. The tables developed here are for the $2, $3, and $5 tables for various sized bankrolls. You do not have to memorize or study all the tables since your bankroll will determine which tables apply to you. To simplify the betting formula just two zones are used. Zone 1 comprises the first half of the cards dealt from the shoe and in front of the cut card. In Zone 2, then, are the remaining cards left in the shoe. This is where your observation of the discard tray comes in handy. With a little practice, you will be able to tell with a high degree of accuracy which zone your table is in. Further, when you are not playing, it is a good idea to roam about the blackjack area, observing dealers in action. Note the discard trays. Estimate from the tray which zone the table is in. Also, pay attention to where the dealer places the cut card.

These little exercises will prove very profitable and certainly beats hanging around the roulette wheel which profits one not at all, or listening to some rock group whose only reason for existence is to distract serious players from their relentless pursuit of the buck. The running count is far more important for betting purposes in Zone 2 than in Zone 1 since the closer we come to the end of the shoe, the more valid is our count, so we increase our bets by fifty percent in Zone 2 for the same running count. All running count (RC) figures are positive or plus counts, since we bet only the minimum on negative counts.

TABLE 1

$500 bankroll. $2 Table.   Betting range 5 to 1.

ZONE 1			ZONE 2	
RC	BET		RC	BET
2	$2.00		2	$3.00
3	3.00		3	4.50
4	4.00		4	6.00
5	5.00		5	7.50
6	5.00		6	9.00
7	5.00		7	10.00
8	5.00		8	10.00

Note: Maximum bet in Zone 1 is $5.00; maximum bet in Zone 2 is $10.00.

TABLE 2

$500 bankroll. $3 Table.   Betting range 4 to 1.

ZONE 1			ZONE 2	
RC	BET		RC	BET
3	$3.00		3	$4.50
4	4.00		4	6.00
5	5.00		5	7.50
6	6.00		6	9.00
7	7.00		7	10.50
8	8.00		8	12.00

TABLE 3

$500 bankroll. $5 Table.   Betting range 3 to 1.

ZONE 1			ZONE 2	
RC	BET		RC	BET
5	$5.00		5	$7.50
6	6.00		6	9.00
7	7.00		7	10.00
8	8.00		8	12.00
9	9.00		9	13.00
10	10.00		10	15.00

Note: There is a higher degree of risk using Table 3 than the previous two. Also, the betting spread, of necessity, is less than Tables 1 and 2. With a $500 bankroll use this Table *only* if there are no $2 or $3 tables available and you feel you *must* play blackjack.

TABLE 4

$750 bankroll. $2 Table.   Betting range 7½ to 1.

ZONE 1		ZONE 3	
RC	BET	RC	BET
2	$2.00	2	$3.00
3	3.00	3	4.50
4	4.00	4	6.00
5	5.00	5	7.50
6	6.00	6	9.00
7	7.00	7	10.00
8	8.00	8	12.00
9	9.00	9	14.00
10	10.00	10	15.00

TABLE 5

$750 bankroll. $3 Table.   Betting range 5 to 1.

ZONE 1		ZONE 2	
RC	BET	RC	BET
3	$3.00	3	$4.50
4	4.00	4	6.00
5	5.00	5	7.50
6	6.00	6	9.00
7	7.00	7	10.00
8	8.00	8	12.00
9	9.00	9	14.00
10	10.00	10	15.00

TABLE 6

$750 bankroll. $5 Table.   Betting range 4 to 1.

ZONE 1		ZONE 2	
RC	BET	RC	BET
5	$5.00	5	$7.50
6	6.00	6	9.00
7	7.00	7	10.00
8	8.00	8	12.00
9	9.00	9	14.00

10	10.00	10	15.00
11	11.00	11	17.00
12	12.00	12	18.00
13	13.00	13	20.00

TABLE 7

$1000 bankroll. $3 Table.   Betting range 7.3 to 1.

ZONE 1		ZONE 2	
RC	BET	RC	BET
3	$3.00	3	$4.50
4	4.00	4	6.00
5	5.00	5	7.50
6	6.00	6	9.00
7	7.00	7	10.00
8	8.00	8	12.00
9	9.00	9	14.00
10	10.00	10	15.00
11	11.00	11	17.00
12	12.00	12	18.00
13	13.00	13	20.00
14	14.00	14	21.00
15	15.00	15	22.00

TABLE 8

$1000 bankroll. $5 Table.   Betting range 4.6 to 1.

ZONE 1		ZONE 2	
RC	BET	RC	BET
5	$5.00	5	$7.50
6	6.00	6	9.00
7	7.00	7	10.00
8	8.00	8	12.00
9	9.00	9	14.00
10	10.00	10	15.00
11	11.00	11	17.00
12	12.00	12	18.00
13	13.00	13	20.00
14	14.00	14	21.00
15	15.00	15	23.00

So much for the tables. These should satisfy everyone but

the high rollers, who with their kind of money, can devise their own.

Most people are not very comfortable with math. When confronted with tables of figures, it is American to panic. Don't! There is nothing complicated or difficult about these tables. They do not have to be analyzed, studied or memorized since there is a simple explanation for the way they are put together. Just bear in mind that the running count of 3 is always a plus 3. Also remember, if the count is negative, a minimum bet is placed. Most of the time you will be playing with a minimum bet since the count has to be at least a +2 before you increase your bet. A count of +12, for example, is rare. Nice, but rare.

Now for some generalities. You will note that in Zone 1, in most cases, you bet $1 per point. In Zone 2, the bet is 1 per point plus fifty percent. You should also note that the lower minimum tables offer the most desirable betting range. And please remember: The greater the spread, the greater your chances of going home a winner.

Look at Table 1 which shows the proper bet at a $2 table with a bankroll of $500 in a 6-deck game. In a 6-deck game, approximately 4½ decks are used—the remaining 1½ decks will rest forever behind the cut card. Zone 1 permits a maximum bet of only $5.00, no matter how positive the running count. Zone 2, however, allows a maximum bet of $10.00 since the running count becomes increasingly important as the shoe is played out. To illustrate, if only ten cards remain in the shoe and the running count is +10, then, theoretically, every remaining card must be a 10 or an ace.

Every table uses this same logic with slight variations to simplify the amount to be wagered. Looking at Table 3, for example, the correct bet in Zone 2 with a running count of 7 is given as $10.00. Since Zone 1 indicates a $7.00 bet for a running count of 7, Zone 2 should show $10.50 as the proper bet. Such a bet is perfectly correct and the one called for, but it just makes good sense to simplify the bet to two red chips.

Note, too, that in looking over the tables, the lower the minimum bet for the various sized bankrolls, the greater the betting range will be. This is the essence of card counting. The greater the betting range, the greater the odds in favor of the player. This point cannot be stressed too often. A sad reality of life, however, is that most of the time you will be playing with a neutral or negative count. So when the count becomes highly positive move out your chips and enjoy.

A reality of the casino scene is the scarcity of $2 and $3 tables. Casino policy, and this includes all of them, discriminates against the player with a limited bankroll. Their policy, in effect, compels such a player to sit at a $5 table where his betting range is somewhat limited. In addition, he may feel uncomfortable at this table and hesitate to make the proper size bet. To illustrate: The correct bet at a $5 table with a bankroll of $500 with a count of +10 in Zone 2 is $15. The player is dealt a pair of 8's, so he splits with $30 riding on the hand. He receives a 3 and a 10 from the dealer. He doubles-down on the 8 and 3 and is now risking $45 or nine percent of his bankroll. So, to play this hand the way it should be played takes the sort of courage that many of us do not have. Therefore, if you have a very modest bankroll, restrict your playing to the morning and early afternoon hours when your chances of having a good time, which means winning, are so much better.

So, before you take your bankroll to your favorite casino, look at the tables. You know what your bankroll is, so jot down if you wish, the tables you will be using. And, just one word of caution: whatever the size of your bankroll, do not bring the entire amount with you. Take half. And never risk the half you do take. Determine how much you are prepared to lose and stand by your decision. This way you will never go broke and the palms of your hands will never become sweaty. Although it is important to approach the casino with confidence and a positive attitude, a fact of life is there *are* times when you will lose. Ken Uston, perhaps the greatest of them all, claimed he lost forty-two percent of the time he played. Or to conclude on a more positive note, he wins fifty-eight percent of the time.

Due to the importance of this chapter, let's summarize the highlights:

- To become a successful blackjack player, proper money management is essential.
- In Zone 1, bet $1.00 per running count. In Zone 2, bet $1.00 per running count plus 50 percent.
- Always, especially if a beginner, play at the lowest minimum table available.
- The wider the betting spread, the better the chance for success.
- If possible, confine casino visits to the morning and early afternoon hours from Monday to Friday. Forget playing on weekends and holidays.
- Never bring more than one-half your bankroll to the casino.

CHAPTER 9

Back Counting

The title of this chapter is a bit misleading. Back counting is not the fun you may think it is since it has nothing to do with counting backs on the beach or anywhere else. It is simply a blackjack technique designed to put more winnings into your pocket.

An important fact: in a typical one-hour blackjack session, less than half that time will be productive or favorable to the player. Most of the time will be spent playing negative, neutral or low positive counts. Wouldn't it be nice then if you could save your money for only strong positive rounds? You can. And there are two ways you can do this. One is to stand behind the players at a table and count when a new shoe is starting. But don't waste time needlessly. Walk around the blackjack area and you're almost sure to see a shuffle in progress. Or, if not, look at the discard trays. An almost full tray means, of course, a new shoe will begin shortly.

If the shoe becomes very positive, a plus 6 or higher, take a seat and play as long as conditions remain favorable. When things take a turn for the worse, get up and leave. Look for another positive table and continue to play as long as you are counting sizeable plusses. Have chips, will travel.

You will not, of course, play as many rounds as you would by playing the more conventional way. But you *will* be playing only favorable rounds. And you will always have the odds in your favor. This technique is called "Wonging it" named for Stanford Wong, a professional blackjack player and writer who pioneered this method of extracting casino funds without the benefit of a gun.

Since you don't plan to spend much time at any one table, it will not be a great sacrifice on your part to stand while playing. There are seven playing positions at each table, but often only six players since the seats are crammed so close together. So edge yourself in and place your bets. Chances are, the casino personnel will think you're a loser since most standees are gamblers down on their luck who like to take a shot or two at a number of tables. They would rather donate their last few chips to the house than refund them at the cashier's cage.

And there is yet another way to outwit the casinos by playing only favorable rounds. A variation on the theme just described. Again, walk around the blackjack tables (these techniques are good for the waistline) but this time don't bother to look for a new shoe. Just scan the cards. Whenever you see a large number of low cards exposed, give them a quick count and take your seat immediately. Play as long as the count remains favorable. This is a very nice way to meet new dealers and see what all the pit bosses are wearing.

These are both powerful techniques almost certain to produce winning sessions. But now for the bad news. Neither of these methods will work for the $2 and $3 bettor for the obvious reason that your chances of sitting at a low-minimum table at a moment's notice are just about nil. However, this should not disturb the card counter. Since you will be playing only strongly positive rounds, your bets should never be less than $5. And most of the time, finding $5 tables should present no problem.

So expand your blackjack horizons. Try these techniques to add a little flavor and variety to your game. If you are a $2 or $3 bettor, you can "Wong it" whenever the minimum is raised. A constant complaint of the small bettor who arrives via bus is that there are no $2 or $3 tables available after 1:00 PM and the bus home doesn't depart until 4:30. Well, if this is your complaint, here is something to try. The only bad feature with back counting is that you won't have time to order a coffee or soda while at the blackjack table. But even in the casinos, you can't have everything. Something has to be sacrificed in the interest of good odds.

CHAPTER 10

Casino Comportment

This chapter is designed to make you feel at ease in a casino. It will build your self-confidence by extending a few hints on how to comport yourself at a blackjack table. It may be acceptable to be a dummy at bridge, but never at blackjack. Be a professional.

If you are having a losing session, have no fears. The casino loves you, the pit boss loves you, and the dealer loves you. You are more than welcome. But if you're doing what every good card counter is expected to be doing—winning—then you should be aware that you're persona non grata.

The dealer and the pit boss know how many chips you buy. Every time you buy chips, the dealer will call out, "changing fifty" or whatever the amount for two reasons: to keep the dealer honest and to call attention to the amount of chips going in your direction.

Now, one purpose of this chapter is to teach you how to foil the casinos. A lesson in how to be devious. How to acquire bad habits, like being sloppy. Neatness does count in some areas of life but not in blackjack. Most players, unfortunately for them, are neat. They keep their chips in neat little stacks according to denomination. Don't! This makes it too easy for the pit boss to see how well you are doing at a glance. Pile your chips in a heap so it is impossible for the house to see how successful you are.

Also, it is wise to place some of your winnings in your pocket from time to time, although it is not advisable to en-

47

gage in this bit of chicanery while the pit boss is watching. And if you plan to stay in Atlantic City for more than one day, don't cash all your chips in—save some for the next day's play. Or, if you plan to play at another table, hold onto your chips. Then only you will know how much of a winner you are.

Here are a few behavioral tips that may make your casino visits more profitable: First, some tips on tipping. Be very sparing in handing out tips (called tokes in the trade) to your dealer. And if you ever feel compelled to tip, make sure that the pit boss sees you. You'll look like the typical gambler. Since the dealer cannot help you in any way, except perhaps in giving a good cut, tipping him is a foolish expenditure. And I've yet to see a dealer tip a friendly player.

It is okay to tip the cocktail waitress. You should. Since it is illegal to sell drinks at the gaming tables, all drinks are on the house. A card counter should never order an intoxicating drink while playing. Only if you plan to stop playing within a half-hour should you think drink. A dollar tip for any drink is acceptable and for coffee or juice a fifty-cent tip will not get you a big smile, but at least you won't get the evil eye.

When a shoe is started, the dealer discards the first card out of the shoe. This is called the burn card. Occasionally, a friendly dealer will show the burn card, but that doesn't happen often. If a player asks to see this card, the rules say the dealer must show it. And every time a dealer is relieved, the new dealer discards the next card out of the shoe.

Use hand signals since the rules say you must. And use them correctly. Too many players give questionable signals that slow up play causing grief to the dealer and annoyance for the others at the table. Do not lean back in your seat and give the signals close to the chest. Get your hands out where they can be seen and make clear and decisive signals.

Keep your hands away from your bet or you will be told to do so. Never, *never* touch the cards if you want to split or for any other reason. This is another rule that is strictly enforced.

When you place a bet of two or more colors, place the lower-priced chip on top or the dealer will be forced to do it for you. Also, arrange your chips in one pile in the betting circle no matter how many chips you are betting.

If the person sitting next to you is a chatterbox, ignore him. Don't be a nice guy. Be rude. You can't count and hold a coversation at the same time. Wait for the shuffle if you have something that must be said.

Act the part of a gambler if it is within you. Show some emotion. Thump the table once in a while when the dealer draws a 21 to top your 20. Make the table come alive. Don't act like the cool, calculating card counter that you are.

If you observe these guidelines you will enjoy the game considerably more.

CHAPTER 11

Cheating

When we speak of cheating at blackjack, we usually have only one thought in mind: how it is possible for the casinos to cheat their customers. But cheating is a two-way street. There are any number of people who dream up ingenious ways to defraud the house. Just recently, the casinos prosecuted a large organized group that was bringing home huge winnings from the slot machines. Yes, the lowly slots were finally paying off! So the casinos *knew* there had to be some hanky-panky. After months of careful investigation, the security force learned that the group was playing with wires. A coin was attached to a thin, almost invisible wire that was inserted far enough into the machine to activate the plums and cherries.

And credit scams of less than a million dollars are hardly newsworthy these days. But the casinos themselves must accept part of the blame with their ultra-liberal credit policies. Caesars, for example, which has the most liberal credit policy of any Atlantic City casino, extended more than $500 million in credit since opening in June 1979. Of this amount they figure from 2-2 1/2 percent is uncollectable, which amounts to somewhere between $10 and $12 million down the drain. That is a lot of money even in these inflationary times.

The Philadelphia Inquirer carried a story in September 1981 about a $16,000 a year corrections officer who was extended a $60,000 credit line at Caesars Regency and another $30,000 at Bally's Park Place. Needless to say, this gambler—

as gamblers are prone to do—ran into a streak of bad luck. He now has a permanent job washing dishes for Caesars and Bally's.

But our concern is not with individuals cheating the casinos. The casinos are well able to take care of themselves. In the good old days in Nevada when the casinos caught a gambler cheating the house, he was taken for a ride in the desert. There, his wrists were promptly broken. Today, the casinos use more sophisticated, if duller, ways to deal with the culprit. The question we would like answered is: Are the casinos cheating the public? Are they really above suspicion? Almost everyone believes the casinos are 100 percent honest. There is too much at stake, they reason, for a house to risk losing its license. True, you will never find a marked card, a second-dealing shoe, or loaded dice at an Atlantic City casino since these all provide prima facie evidence that can be used in court.

However, when you are playing perfect basic strategy and lose eight consecutive rounds, you tend to pay a little more attention to the dealer. *Is* he cheating? And if so, *how*? It is fairly easy for a dealer to cheat with a hand-held deck by second-dealing, especially if the casino uses borderless Bee cards. In Nevada, good "mechanics" (cheating dealers) are able to deal not only a second card, but a third card or bottom card. They are masters of their trade. But, how is it possible for a dealer to cheat in a shoe game?

Well, one way is by "clumping" or keeping a clump or slug of high cards together so they are never put into play. This is done by an inadequate shuffle when new cards are put into play and are destined to remain safely behind the cut card as long as the dealer continues to employ an inadequate shuffle. This infraction leveled at one Atlantic City casino has been brought to the attention of the New Jersey Casino Control Commission. So, anytime a counter has too many high plus counts when the shoes are completed, he should start thinking "clump" and find another dealer.

Another way for the dealer to cheat is by "high-lowing" or interspersing high and low cards as he scoops them up after the hand is played. Whenever you are dealt an abnormally high percentage of high-low cards such as 10,2; 9,3; 10,4; 10,5, leave the table. Perhaps the dealer is honest, but don't bet on it.

Many dealers don't know what "clumping" and "high-lowing" are. Yet, they may be just as dishonest in more unimaginative ways. Lazy dishonesty. Like taking your money on a push or paying even money instead of 3 for 2 on a blackjack. Especially watch the pay-out when you have four or five card hands including an ace or two. Don't rely on the dealer to add your hand correctly.

Atlantic City casinos are as honest as any other big business enterprise. They take great pains to prove to the public (and the New Jersey Casino Control Commission) that they operate a lily-white game. Observe, for example, the ritual of starting up a blackjack table. The faces and then the backs of the cards are carefully inspected by the dealer. Next, the decks are laid out in sequence for all to see. The okay is given by the pit boss. Then much is made of mixing up all the cards, the dealer running his hands through and around the mound of cards like a master chef preparing a sumptuous meal for some very important people.

Most dealers are about as honest as your corner butcher. Perhaps a little less so, since most of them do not intend to remain at the old stand for any long period of time. Dealing is a boring, monotonous job, hard on the feet. But there is a certain aura of glamour and the sweet scent of money to compensate. Although dealers work for minimum wage, the income they receive in tokes can be considerable. And in Atlantic City, they don't even have to smile or be nice. Unlike Vegas, the tokes they receive from their grateful public are divied up and shared equally by all. So, unlike your corner butcher, you do not have to watch for the thumb on the scale for short weight. However, you had better watch very carefully at pay-out time for short change.

CHAPTER 12

Advanced Basic Strategy

As mentioned earlier, there is only *one* basic strategy for the Atlantic City blackjack rules. But, as with almost every rule, there are the exceptions. For the basic strategy player there are none, but the card counter can benefit by deviating from the norm depending on the count. That's why it's nice to be a card counter. Not only does he vary his bets, but he can also vary his play.

And this is the way it works. When the shoe is positive, the counter should stand more often since there is an abnormally high percentage of 10's remaining in the shoe. The counter should double-down more because he stands a greater chance of drawing a high card and the dealer has a greater chance of breaking when he hits a stiff hand. And because the dealer is more likely to break, the counter should split pairs more often.

When the shoe is negative, the counter quite naturally takes the opposite view. He will hit more often since there is a high percentage of low cards remaining in the shoe. He will double-down less often since he has a greater chance of drawing a low card and the dealer is less likely to break. And he will split pairs less often since, again, he is more likely to draw low cards and the dealer is less likely to break.

If you think about this concept, you will see why it makes sense. However, if you find it too confusing to put into use, forget it. The important thing is to play as nearly errorless blackjack as possible. And the small advantage that you gain by varying basic strategy will be lost if you fail to master the variations.

For the bold, here are some variations that will increase your winnings:

PLAYER'S HAND	DEALER'S UP-CARD	DECISION
12	4	Stand on 0 or + Hit on -
16	10	Stand on 0 or + Hit on -
3,3	2	Split on 0 or + Hit on -
9,4	2	Stand on 0 or + Hit on -
7,2	2	Double on 0 or + Hit on -
4,4	5/6	Split on 0 or + Hit on -
A,2	5	Double on 0 or + Hit on -
A,7	2	Double on 0 or + Stand on -
A,7	A	Stand on 0 or + Hit on -
A,8	6	Double on 0 or + Stand on -

These 10 basic strategy variations will help in a small way to increase the counter's bankroll. The most important variation is the player's decision to stand on 16 against the dealer's 10 when the count is 0 or plus since this decision is faced so many times during a blackjack session. So for those who do not wish to include all these variations in their repertoire, at

56   *Advanced Basic Strategy*

least add the player's hand of 16 against the dealer's 10.

So the card counter not only has the advantage of money management (increasing his bets when conditions are favorable), he also can vary his strategy according to the contents of the shoe. As Damon Runyon once remarked, "The race is not always to the swift, nor the battle to the strong—but that's the way to bet."

CHAPTER 13

Advanced Play

Despite whatever personal problems beset your life, you have arrived to an enviable position. Now you belong to a very select group that has an edge over the casinos. You can sit at the blackjack tables with an air of confidence and rightfully feel superior to the other players.

This distinction was earned. You learned basic strategy and practiced it until it has become second-nature. There are no more moments of indecision. You practiced your card counting drills faithfully so that counting is no longer a chore. The fastest dealer in Atlantic City does not intimidate you.

But most important of all—you are winning. Ever wonder how your winnings compare with other card counters? Well, if you have a casino bankroll of $800 with a playing bankroll of $400 (your playing bankroll should be one-half your casino bankroll), you should show a profit of about $3 an hour. Yes, $3 per hour! Less than minimum wage. With a casino bankroll of $1500, you can expect to make $5 an hour. Not exactly a handsome sum either, but remember that your typical blackjack player is donating somewhere between six and fifteen percent of his bankroll to the casinos. No one ever said playing blackjack was an easy way to turn a buck.

However, if you're interested in higher blackjack earnings and are willing to devote the time and effort to this cause, there are a couple of ways to increase your hourly profit.

One way is to become more sophisticated in your counting techniques. You are now working with the one-level, plus/

minus 1, using a running count. This system, as you've discovered, is easy to learn and quite effective. It is not, however, the *most* effective. There are multi-level count systems that assign values greater than plus or minus 1, using a true count instead of a running count and with a separate count of aces. A word of caution is in order here. While it is true that multi-level count systems increase the player's chances of winning, it is also true that a greater number of errors, far greater than many suppose, are made in counting by overly-ambitious players. It is more profitable to count accurately with a one-level system than to make an error or two an hour using a more powerful system.

The best way to learn about these highly sophisticated counting techniques is to take an advanced course at a reputable blackjack school. There may be one in your area and, if not, some have correspondence courses. This route is the best, the fastest, and the easiest. If, however, you are cheap and do not wish to risk the money (these courses are rather expensive, charging fees of $400 to $600), then the information can be gotten from the many books written on the subject. Some caveats about the book route: many still in print are almost completely obsolete, and most books were published before Atlantic City blackjack came on the scene. Further, many readers often misinterpret the author's meaning or intention. If the subject happens to be sociology, no great harm is done by a misreading of the text. A misreading of a blackjack text could result in a financial horror. Also, any intelligent questions you would like to ask have to go unanswered.

Another way to enhance your earnings is to become acquainted with team play. Here you pool your bankroll with other players of equal ability. Or superior ability if you're lucky. A team, for practical reasons, usually consists of from three to six players, which means each player's bankroll is increased three to six times. To go back to the example used earlier, the $400 bankroll producing a $3 hourly win magically becomes $12 with a team of four players. Again, not really a handsome sum, but at least respectable. And with four team players, each with an ante of $750, you can expect to win about $20 an hour. The reason for this seemingly improbable surge in winnings is that in pooling your money, you'll be playing with a much larger bankroll plus a far greater betting spread.

Moreover, team play is a lot more fun for most players than playing alone. And the financial rewards outweigh its obvious shortcomings. The most obvious, naturally, is dishonesty. However, a dishonest team member will soon be discovered. But just in the interest of acceptable business practices, a polygraph should be available. Another shortcoming might be the poor performance by a member of your team. Usually this is the result of a player's failure to do his homework—neglecting his card drills and flash cards. Or perhaps he may be imbibing on the job. Whatever the reason, the team may elect to give him a pink slip. Every player will experience a losing streak. But it is fairly easy to recognize the difference between a losing streak and consistently poor play.

One final and quite practical reason that team play has not become more widespread is the difficulty in assembling a group of players of high caliber to agree to pool their resources. Do you know of any counters who play as well as you do?

Most players, however, do not wish to go on to advanced play since it does take total commitment. And it is not for the $3 and $5 bettor. But if you're prepared to spend the time, the effort and the money, it can be quite profitable. There are players who have blackjack winnings of six figures plus. So, if you wish to go on to become a professional, good luck and good winnings.

CHAPTER 14

Is Card Counting for Everyone?

As you know by now, card counting is work. A counter enters a casino as a business man enters his office He is there to make a profit and any enjoyment he has doing so is coincidental. If you look upon your visit to the casino as a lark, then you are not the stuff from which card counters are made.

But no apologies are in order. It is not necessary to be a card counter to take your place at the blackjack table and play a decent game. Of course, the counter has an edge on the casino while the basic strategy player does not. But there are other considerations of even greater importance than the difference between a few percentage points for or against the player. If you plan to visit the casinos just a few times a year, your time-consuming investment in card drills will not pay off. If you do not enjoy the card drills and trying to improve upon your drill times, then the discipline of counting is not for you. And if you are a social animal and can't have an amicable time without good conversation and hoisting a few drinks, forget card counting. There is no stigma attached to being a basic strategy player. On the contrary, you will be playing a far better game than the others seated at your table.

The only tools the basic strategy player needs are a set of flash cards and a deck of playing cards. The night before you visit the casino bone up. Run through your flash cards and deal out 3- to 7-hand games. Especially practice soft hands since these are the most difficult and offer so many opportunities to double-down.

The money management charts have no meaning for the basic strategy player. So how much to bet? Whatever amount provides you with a little excitement. And, of course, never bet more than you can afford to lose. For the most part you will be a flat bettor. The trap most players set for themselves is increasing their bets when losing. They chase their losses. Don't ever try to double up to recoup your losses. This betting strategy will only end in disaster. Smart players increase their bets when they're ahead, not behind. The ultimate is tossing a $50 bill on the table, and in a short time, pocketing the $50 in chips and spending the rest of the session playing with house money.

A basic strategy player doesn't need to concern himself with the dealer. Any dealer will do. He can be the fastest, slickest one in the East, mumble or not even call out the count, and wear a five-carat sparkler that threatens your retina. Who cares?

However, if you visit the casinos ten or more times a year, you should give card counting some serious thought. Your investment in time will certainly pay off. Like everything in life, that in which we excel we enjoy. And a counter will excel in the long run. No matter how easily a loss is shrugged off, losing does not elevate the spirit. Just as a good round of golf keeps us coming back to the first tee, a winning session at the blackjack tables encourages us to pay an early return to the casino. No one throws his golf clubs away after a good round.

There are certain personality traits that most counters have. Among these are a strong ego, a competitive drive, self-discipline and, in some, a desire to go on to become a professional blackjack player. A worthy aim. There are, perhaps, only about a hundred professional blackjack players at any one time in Vegas. No one has ever tried to count the number in Atlantic City, but there is always room for one more.

Know yourself. If you have some of the above-mentioned traits, you may be on your way to becoming a good card counter. There is no such thing, incidentally, as a bad card counter. It's like being pregnant; you can't be a little pregnant. So either you're a good counter or you can't count. Of course, there are various levels of blackjack systems ranging from one-level to multi-level, from a fairly simple hi-low to the sophisticated advanced point count, but the winning percentages do not vary that greatly. A counter using the one-level, hi-low method has a powerful system and will win in the long run.

The important thing is to, like a Boy Scout, be prepared. Come to the casino with the knowlege that the house has a six to fifteen percent advantage over the free-wheeling, fun-loving rube who thinks that all he needs is a little bit of luck to go home a winner. So at the very least, use basic strategy and give the house a run for its money.

To summarize: Determine which type of player you would like to be—an expert or a social player. If you do not plan to spend much time at the casinos, and look upon your infrequent visits as just going out for a good time, then you are a social player. Learn basic strategy and retain what you have learned by practicing card drills and running through your flash cards before your visit. However, if you plan to visit the casinos at least ten times a year, have the self-discipline to learn basic strategy until it becomes second nature, and possess a strong competitive drive, then you have the characteristics of a card counter. And as a counter, you will be a member of an elite corps.

CHAPTER 15

The History of Blackjack at Atlantic City

Not too long ago, Atlantic City blackjack was the best game to be found anywhere in the world. The rules established by the New Jersey Rules Commission permitting the player to split on any pair, to double-down on any two cards, to double-down after splitting a pair, and requiring the dealer to stand on a soft 17 were all designed to be favorable to the player. But the biggest inducement of all was early surrender, a rule that permitted the player to surrender his hand and one-half his original bet if he believed he held a losing hand. So, even if the dealer had a blackjack, the player would lose only one-half his original bet. Many casinos in other areas permit late surrender, which does not allow the player to surrender if the dealer has blackjack.

There was a practical reason for the Commission to set up these lenient rules. The gaming industry was new to the East Coast. Casinos from all over the world were watching with more than passing interest the pioneer casino, Resorts International, which opened its doors to the public on May 26, 1978. As history shows, Resorts International proved to be an enormous success, prompting other casinos to go ahead with building plans. Three years later, May of 1981, seven casinos were in operation with two more, the Claridge and the Tropicana, nearing completion.

Then something happened in that lovely month of May.

The casinos decided that their blackjack profits were not as high as they would like, placing the blame primarily on the early surrender rule. "It has to go!" they chorused as in a single voice. But what they didn't realize was that this rule enticed great numbers of would-be blackjack players who hadn't the faintest idea of how to apply this rule to their advantage. In any event, the casinos were determined that the rule must go. A spokesman for the Atlantic City Casino Hotel Association, David Gardner, said, "New Jersey has the most favorable rules in the world as far as the player goes. This is a situation that has to change." It was changed and quickly! By May 27, 1981, the early surrender rule was quite dead and unlike the phoenix will probably never rise from the ashes.

During the month of July of that year quite a battle was waged to restore the early surrender rule, led by Ken Uston and New Jersey Assemblyman Dennis Riley. Lawmaker Riley holds the dubious distinction of being tossed out of two casinos for allegedly counting cards. To support the return of the rule, there were a protest march along the boardwalk from The Golden Nugget to Resorts International, a boycott of the blackjack tables, and a series of articles published in the now defunct *Philadelphia Bulletin* in favor of early surrender, written by blackjack expert, Jerry L. Patterson. There was one hollow victory. On July 15, the Casino Control Commission agreed with Ken Uston that there was a procedural error—failure to give thirty days public notice and conduct a hearing—in its May ruling suspending the surrender rule and ordered the surrender rule reinstated at 10:00 A.M. on July 17.

So the card counters and basic strategy players dusted off their basic strategy ponies to refresh their memories of when to surrender. But the victory was short-lived—lasting about twenty-four hours. The next day, the Casino Control Commission reversed itself and voted 3-1 to again abolish the surrender option. After listening to three hours of testimony by lawyers representing the casino industry, the Commission agreed that an "emergency" existed and that early surrender would result in tremendous financial losses to the present casinos and would discourage plans for future casinos planning to open their doors in Atlantic City. Predictably, the fickle hand of the Commission succumbed to industry pressure.

As a rationale for abolishing the early surrender rule, the Atlantic City Casino Hotel Association hired the Princeton consulting firm of Econ, Inc., to study the card counters advantage and other aspects of the game of blackjack.

Econ came up with some pretty strange findings. An "aggressive" card counter, they concluded, enjoyed a 4.38 percent advantage over the house. If only this were so! By their definition, an "aggressive" card counter was one who employed a wide betting range without fear of being ousted by the casino. Twenty years study of millions of computerized hands indicated the counter had an edge of only 1 1/2-2 percent over the house. And this assumed that the player was employing perfect basic strategy, counting accurately, and making use of sophisticated money management techniques.

Among other strange findings presented to the casinos by Econ were that 27 percent of Atlantic City blackjack players used basic strategy and that one out of every 30 players was a card counter. Let's not say that the firm was somewhat inaccurate in its reporting, but it was hired by the Atlantic City Casino Hotel Association with an eye towards finding a rationale for changing the rules of blackjack to make the odds more favorable to the casinos.

It may seem at this point that the year 1981 is being covered ad nauseum. In defense, it can be safely stated that in the short history of blackjack at Atlantic City, that was a pivotal year. In the world of blackjack not much happened before that fateful year and not much of real significance has happened since. But read on. Casino management is never content with the status quo.

There were other measures the casinos were taking to make life difficult for blackjack players. If the casinos did not welcome blackjack players, what move could be more simple than to just remove the tables? And that is exactly what the casinos did. Blackjack tables were replaced with more profitable craps tables and roulette and Big Six wheels. The casinos claimed they made this move because women prefer roulette and craps. Women prefer craps over blackjack? You know that's a lot of crap!

So, the unwelcome mat for blackjack players was out. During the first two months of 1981, the six casinos operating in this period got rid of thirty-two tables. Caesars Boardwalk Regency replaced eight blackjack tables with roulette and craps tables. Caesars Vice-President Larry J. Woolf explained their move into roulette: "A novice can sit down and play black or red. It's not too complicated, good for beginners. By contrast, in Nevada we're dealing with a gaming-educated market. The people have acquired a skill. Here, we're doing some educating." He failed to mention that the casino's advantage at roulette is much higher than blackjack. So much for the role of Caesars in education.

Bally's Park Place Casino dropped sixteen blackjack tables and replaced them with four craps tables, two roulette tables and two Big Six wheels. The Big Six wheels are impulse items placed strategically near the exits to siphon off any extra cash that the customer doesn't need for parking fees or gasoline. Their claim to fame is their low payoff. And the roulette wheels are not noted for their generosity, either. For example, the August 1981 count for the roulette tables at Bally's Park Place revealed the total amount bet for that month was $3,696,183 with a casino win of $1,252,913. Not bad. By far, the most favorable roulette odds at Atlantic City were given by Playboy with their much-publicized single O. The other casinos used a double O, which did not help the player very much as we shall see. For the same month, the total amount bet on the roulette wheels at Playboy totaled $4,037,464 with a total win of only $698,944. What a difference an O can make! The casino win per $100 wagered at Bally's was $33.90 for that month, while the casino win per $100 wagered at

Playboy was $17.30. So the lesson is, if you *must* play rou-
lette, go to a casino that features the single O.

Resorts International dropped two blackjack tables and re-
placed them with two Big Six wheels. Resorts spokesman Phil
Weschler insisted there was no significance to the change.
Just a passing whim, no doubt.

The Golden Nugget, which in March 1981, decided to drop
four to six blackjack tables, wound up by replacing eight with
roulette wheels and craps tables. Explained casino manager,
Bucky Howard: "With roulette, when you hit, you win a lot.
The game is a sort of baby-sitter... make that playground
... for the ladies." Isn't it comforting how the casinos cater to
the ladies?

So there appears to be a nearly unanimous feeling in casino
management that craps, roulette and the Big Six are good for
the public and that blackjack is a necessary evil. The only two
casino activities not mentioned by the brass are baccarat and
the slot machines. The high-roller game and the blue-collar
pastime. Since there are relatively few high-rollers attracted
to Atlantic City, two or three baccarat tables per casino are all
that are needed. And since many blue collar types are drawn
to the Atlantic City casinos, there is a disportionate amount of
space provided for the slots. Not surprisingly, Bally's Park
Place headed all other casinos in the number of slot machines
with 1,686. After all, Bally's manufactures the little one-
armed bandits. The smallest casino, the Claridge, with 30,000
square feet, had 862 slot machines. Perhaps in the future
there will be the ultimate casino featuring nothing but slot
machines. It will be the envy of the other casinos.

So much for what has actually developed within the short
space of a few years—the nullifying of what was once the best
blackjack game in the world to a much less desirable one,
although one that is still beatable. Were the casinos now satis-
fied with the current blackjack rules? Of course not.

Now (July 1981) casino management—with the approval of
the Casino Control Commission—began experimenting with

the 8-deck shoe. The cut card was to be placed approximately in the middle of the shoe so that the shuffle will be made after half the cards are played.

Three tables at Resort's International, four at the Golden Nugget and four at Caesars Regency experimented with the 8-deck shoe under Commission supervision. Commission spokesman Ben Borowsky said the 8-deck game might be an alternative if the New Jersey Supreme Court decided that casinos may not bar card counters from playing blackjack. The 8-deck game was introduced and is still used by the majority of the casinos.

In the new game the cut card was placed in the middle of the shoe and a shuffle made when this card turned up. To regain the advantage enjoyed before the adverse rule changes, the serious player employed a number of counter-measures. Among them were: taking insurance when the count is very positive (+10); watching for clumps of high cards in the discard tray and following them through the shuffle; "Wonging it" or back counting and playing only positive shoes. Any or all of these countermeasures may be used to increase the player's edge over the casino. Probably the single most effective method is back counting. And the most efficient way to back count is to head for the Bally-Claridge-Sands complex where almost 200 tables are available within one city block.

The 8-deck middle-of-the-shoe-cut card game lasted several years. Then eventually, the casinos realized that shuffling costs money and began moving the cut card toward the back of the shoe. Now, two casinos employ the 6-deck game, but whether 6- or 8-deck games are played, the cut card is placed in a reasonable spot—about 1 1/2-2 decks from the back of the shoe.

The most devastating measure considered by the casinos was an anti-card counting device called Blackjack 2, manufactured by Vingt et Un (21 for those weak in French) Corporation. This device employs a double shoe containing twelve decks of cards, six red-back decks in one compartment and six blue-back decks in the other. The cards from each side of the shoe are shuffled and dealt separately. The dealer's up-card determines whether red or blue will be dealt. If his up-card is red then red-back cards are dealt to the players; if his up-card is blue, the blue-backs are dealt.

This device would put the card counter out of business. Not only would the counter have to keep two separate counts, he would have to place his bet *before* knowing which color would be dealt. This double shoe might spell not only the end of the card counter but also the end of the game of blackjack at Atlantic City. It took many years for blackjack to reach its present popularity. And Blackjack 2 would change the game from one of skill to one of luck. It is doubtful, how-ever, that the casinos would ever permit their most popular game to be destroyed.

This chapter is not intended to be an indictment of the casinos for wanting to show a profit. As business enterprises, their prime responsibility is to maximize earnings for their stockholders. Our contention is that one facet of their busi-ness—the game of blackjack—is singled out as contributing to whatever woes beset the industry, possibly because it is the easiest game to manipulate. We also believe that poor busi-ness practices, unmanned tables and the dearth of low-mini-mum tables, contribute heavily to profits being less than they would be if better business acumen were exercised.

Just a word or two about management's attitude towards low-minimum tables. And it is one, unfortunately, that applies to all casinos: low-minimum tables, they believe, are neces-sary evils that should be tolerated only during the extremely slow period at the beginning of the day. Raise the minimum, and thereby winnings, as soon as the crowds arrive shortly after noon. This management technique, while seemingly sound, does not work to the advantage of the casino. Many blackjack players, like horse players, are $2 and $3 bettors. If they are prohibited from placing their small bets, they simply will not play. In addition, there are great numbers of players sitting at the low-minimum tables who are wagering bets much higher than the required minimum. And too, there are many players who are not flat bettors but who like to vary their bets depending on whether they are winning or losing. But for whatever perverse reason, the casinos would sooner permit a row of dealers with arms folded to wait for a customer to start the action at a $10 minimum table than operate a busy $3 minimum table.

None of this criticism is intended to imply that the present blackjack rules at Atlantic City are less favorable than the rules that apply in other parts of the gambling world. They are not. Atlantic City blackjack rules are more favorable than the Caribbean rules, particularly Aruba, and most of the European rules. Each casino in Nevada for instance, sets its own rules, and they run the gamut from very favorable to avoid at all costs. And they are constantly changing. The fact that must be underscored, unfortunately, is that the Atlantic City blackjack game, once the best in the world, no longer holds that distinction.

Of course, no one can predict with any degree of accuracy what the future holds for Atlantic City blackjack. However, it is almost certain that with increased competition, the New Jersey Casino Control Commission will relax its rigid control and permit the casinos to regulate themselves in much the same way as they do in Nevada.

Then perhaps, one of the more enterprising casinos might experiment with more liberal rules to see what the effect would be on profits. It would be interesting to determine the impact of a thirty-day relaxation period of the no-surrender option. My guess is that it would attract a record number of blackjack players from all over the world and set new profit records for the casino.

CHAPTER 16

The Future of Atlantic City

At this writing, the future of the gaming industry in Atlantic City is partly cloudy with a promise of sunshine by afternoon. The great wave of optimism that prevailed several years ago has somewhat subsided. When Resorts International was *the* casino, the far-flung gaming industry was eyeing it with great interest and even greater envy. And why not? It proved to be the most successful casino in history taking in $220 million in its first year of operation. So the line to share in the fun, games and profits formed on the right. Glowing predictions of twenty, then thirty casinos in the next ten years were being circulated by the media. It was like the old gold rush days in California with every prospector demanding a stake. Newspapers featured artists' conceptions of casinos stretching the length of the boardwalk with another cluster at Brigantine. Today, eleven years later, there are ten casinos dotting the boardwalk and only two in Brigantine.

Casino expansion has reached a plateau. Why? Well, there are a number of reasons. An important one is the shortage of first-class hotel rooms. Rival Las Vegas has 50,000 rooms; Atlantic City has only 5,000, according to the Atlantic City Casino Association. But help is on the way. Peter F. Tyson, a partner in the accounting firm of Laventhol & Horwath, indicates there are plans for 12,800 new, first-class hotel rooms within the next six years. This, of course, will help the much needed convention business. As it stands now, the casino-hotels have an occupancy rate of about eighty-five percent

71

which is high and discourages those seeking convention sites.

In addition to the planned hotel rooms, four large condos are in the planning stages. These will have an impact of Atlantic City's overall development. Also, just outside of Atlantic City, in places like Absecon and Egg Harbor, 2,000 new rooms are already under construction. Every little bit helps. It must be remembered, however, that plans on a drawing board have a way of falling behind schedule and oftentimes don't materialize at all. Nevertheless, developers are aware of the need for growth and are taking steps to satisfy the need.

Another problem affecting the growth of Atlantic City is the need for transportation. The only way to arrive at a casino is by rubber unless you're a very high roller, in which case the casinos will be happy to fly you in. Yet, there is no major airport for commercial jets.

The trains stopped running years ago. However, there is hope that rail transportation will resume soon. Amtrak is now laying track for the "gambler's express" that will run six express round-trips a day between Philadelphia and Atlantic City and one between New York City and Atlantic City. The project will cost $91.5 million.

Sooner or later it had to happen. With twelve casinos in operation, competition has become a fact of life. Each casino has to actively compete for its share of the market. As in every industry, the strong will survive and prosper the weak go under. In January 1989, three casinos had a lower average daily win than the previous year. One casino, Atlantis, had been in financial trouble from the day it opened, showing losses of about $2 million a month. On November 1, 1985, they were unable to meet their interest payments of $8.9 million on its mortgage bonds. The word "mortgage," by the way, comes from the French word "mort" which means dead. And this is what you are if you don't meet your payments. As a result, that month, Atlantis filed a petition under Chapter 11 of the Federal Bankruptcy Code to protect them from a host of creditors. Their total assets were listed at $170.76 million and total liabilities in excess of $238.82 million including long-term debts totaling $192.52 million. In May 1989, Atlantis ceased operations.

Another reason the casino industry has reached a plateau is the city itself. Most potential visitors have a negative perception of Atlantic City and with good cause. Here exist some of the worst slums in the country, and apart from the boardwalk area, the city is a virtual wasteland.

Finally, the casino industry in Atlantic City is overregulated. Grossly overregulated, which is why Resorts International is anxious to abandon the scene. The Nevada Gaming Control Board has a ratio of about one employee for each casino. In Atlantic City, the Casino Control Commission has a ratio of about 100-1.

The good news is that in the near future the Casino Control Commission will probably relax its tight grip on the industry. For example, the casinos have long petitioned to remain open twenty-four hours instead of closing their doors from 4:00 A.M. during the week and 6:00 A.M. on the weekends to 10:00 A.M. It appears now that their petition may be granted, at least on an experimental basis. The other proposed changes are in casino credit regulations, handing out "comps" and junket operations.

Yet, on the whole, the gaming industry at Atlantic City is in a fairly healthy state—healthier than it would appear from reading the newspapers. Good news, unfortunately, is not the stuff that makes headlines. The winter of 1980-81, when gross earnings dropped nearly 40 percent, rated excellent coverage in the press. September 1984 made the headlines because there was less revenue that month than September 1983. In January 1985, more headlines because the casinos fell short of the predicted $2 billion "win" figure for the year 1984. The "win" was a mere $1.95 billion. And so it goes.

But enough figures for a while. When you start using words like "billion," even high rollers get dizzy. So what is happening now? The latest casino to open is Showboat, Inc. of Las Vegas, which lifted its curtain ahead of schedule. It began operation in the summer of 1987, months ahead of its planned fall opening. The Showboat's concept is togetherness. The owners have a family-oriented operation complete with a 60-lane bowling alley, and since 1989, their operation has been at least as successful as most of the others.

The big success test came in the spring of 1990 when Trump opened his behemoth Taj Mahal Casino-Hotel. This casino looks the biggest and toughest.

There are other planned casino openings in a variety of developmental stages. The Carnival Club on the site of the former Shelburne Hotel was scheduled for a January 1988 opening that got lost in the shuffle. Another planned 1988 opening that never materialized was the L & M Walter Enterprises Casino-Hotel complex to be built at the terminus of the Atlantic City Expressway. Marina area casino, Camelot, is awaiting financing, and finally there is the ever-present Penthouse Hotel-Casino, the construction of which was started years ago but then halted by financial problems. There must be a moral here. Both girlie magazine publishers, Hugh Hefner and Bob Guccione, have had more than their share of problems trying to make a decent living in this gaming capital.

The question is, how many casinos can Atlantic City support? The answer depends on many factors. The problems that beset casino growth were outlined earlier in this chapter. To move upward from its present plateau, additional hotel rooms are a must and cannot be delayed. And transportation has to be improved dramatically, especially for those who live more than 150 miles from the city. Basically, that means getting the trains running and building a decent airport.

Now a word about bus transportation. From Philadelphia the running time to Atlantic City varies between one hour and ninety minutes, and from New York City, about 2½ hours. The much maligned bus is certainly the most visible means of transportation. In 1984, there were 384,358 charter buses carrying 12,241,214 passengers to Atlantic City. Almost without exception the buses are fast, clean and air-conditioned. And almost always, the riders are given a generous supply of freebies, usually more than covering the cost of transportation. The casinos have created, or at least have rejuvenated, a new industry. And a by-product of this industry is the flow of dollars into the hands of travel agencies, drug stores and restaurants that arrange and are departure points for the casino bus trade. If you are allergic to buses and prefer the family car... fine. The roads leading into the gaming capital of the East Coast are excellent. The Atlantic City Expressway is one of the finest roads in the East.

Parking your car is never a problem. All the casinos have adequate parking facilities at reasonable rates. Harrah's Marina, in fact, offers free parking. How long that will last is anyone's guess. Resorts International, with spaces for 4,500 cars, has the largest casino parking lot. Then, there is a sizeable municipal lot on New York Avenue between Atlantic and Pacific Avenues with low parking fees. It is rarely, if ever, full. Pacific Avenue (just one block from the boardwalk) is dotted with reasonably-priced parking areas.

Despite the fact that Atlantic City has twelve casinos as opposed to the ninety in operation at Las Vegas, it has overtaken Vegas in the "win" column and is now the gaming capital of the United States if not the world. For the year 1988, the twelve casinos posted a $2.73 billion "win," a 9.6 percent increase over 1987. Two of the casinos, Caesars and Trump Plaza, each took in more than $300 million for the year, more than any casino has ever collected. Saul Leonard, a gaming analyst for the Philadelphia consulting firm of Laventhol & Horwarth, predicted that 1989 would be an even better year than 1988 with the "win" figure pushing the $3 billion mark.

Eleven of the twelve casinos posted increased "wins" in 1988 over 1987. The sole loser was Bally's Grand. And it was doing so well when it was the Golden Nugget. In 1988, Caesars had the distinction of the largest annual "win" with a record-breaking $307.6 million. Not surprisingly, Atlantis Casino Hotel had the smallest "win," coming in with $84.2 million. Showboat Hotel & Casino posted a whopping forty-three percent increase from its nine-month season in 1987. "Win," it should be added, represents the amount of money the casinos retain after all bets have been paid off. "Win" should not be confused with profit, since operating costs, amortizations and taxes must be deducted.

Interesting too, is the number of annual visitors to Atlantic City. In 1978, the year it all began for the "new" Atlantic City, there were seven million visitors; in 1984, there were 28.5 million. Each year shows a sizeable increase. That's the good news. The bad news is that most visitors stay only one day compared with a four-day stay in Las Vegas. But when the trains start running and the planes start landing, the one-day stay should stretch to a longer one. Although Atlantic City has 53 million people to draw from in a 300-mile radius, in order to support twenty to thirty casinos, it will have to look beyond that radius. At present, according to Marvin Rossman, a gaming analyst with Janney Montgomery Scott Inc. in Philadelphia, the casinos are marketing their product to the same customer base. "In the early days of Atlantic City gambling," said Roffman, "the high end of the business was coming in from the Las Vegas market. If at top-quality player had been gambling six times a year in Vegas, he may have only gone back two times and spent the other four times checking out Atlantic City. Now Vegas has gotten that guy to come back."

The dream of a few years ago of casinos stretching the length of the boardwalk has not yet become a reality. But be patient. Gamblers we will always have with us. As Heywood Broun observed: "The urge to gamble is so universal and its practice so pleasurable that I assume it must be evil."

CHAPTER 17

Selecting Your Casino

Now that you have mastered the game of blackjack, you may wish to spend some time in Atlantic City. This chapter will give you some idea of what the various casinos have to offer.

Each casino has its own ambiance from the smallest, Claridge, to the largest, Showboat. Decor ranges from the tackiness of Showboat and Resorts International to the elegance of Trump Plaza and Trump Castle. In glitz, the prize goes to Bally's Grand. If you prefer a sedate casino try Harrah's Marina. If you like your casino noisy and smoke-filled, there are Resorts International or Caesars. It should be added there are an increasing number of "non-smoking" blackjack tables at all casinos. If your favorite color is burgundy, you will love the TropWorld; if it's deep purple, opt for Bally's Park Place.

As for restaurants, the twelve casinos house ninety-four restaurants ranging from five at Trump Castle to thirteen at Sands, which includes eleven "eateries" in their Food Court. The Food Court is rarely overcrowded and an excellent place for lunch or a snack.

Alphabetically-listed below is information that will come in handy if you plan to stay overnight. Room rates, of course, are subject to change. Be on the lookout for package deals the casinos offer for two or more day visits.

Bally's Grand Casino/Hotel
Boston Ave. at Boardwalk
Telephone: 609-347-7111

Toll-free reservations: 1-800-257-8677
Room rates: Weekdays $110-$130; weekends $110-$130
Summer: Weekdays $110-$130; weekends $110-$130
Recreational facilities: Indoor pool, health club, video arcade
Table games: 94 tables including 57 blackjack, 20 craps
Slot machines: 1,202 machines: 63 5-cent, 788 25-cent, 67 50-cent, 284 $1

Bally's Park Place Casino Hotel
Park Place at Boardwalk
Telephone: 609-340-2000
Toll-free reservation: 1-800-225-5977
Room rates: Weekdays $95-$125; weekends $95-$125
Summer: Weekdays $110-$140; weekends $110-$140
Recreational facilities: Outdoor pool, video arcade
Table games: 117 tables including 76 blackjack, 22 craps
Slot machines: 1,596 machines: 89 5-cent, 1,148 25-cent, 115 50-cent, 244 $1

Caesars Atlantic City Hotel-Casino
Boardwalk at Arkansas Ave.
Telephone: 609-348-4411
Toll-free reservation: 1-800-257-8555
Room rates: Sept. 15, 1988 - June 19, 1989
City view/Standard $120; City view/Deluxe $125; Pool view $125; Ocean view/Standard $150; Tower Deluxe $160
Recreational facilities: Rooftop tennis, platform tennis, pinball arcade, volleyball, domed pool, health spa with equipment room, steam baths, saunas and sun booths plus a 1,100-seat Caesars Maximus Theatre.
Table games: 102 tables including 58 blackjack, 24 craps
Slot machines: 1,681 machines: 108 5-cent, 1,089 25-cent, 206 50-cent, 265 $1, 13 $5

Claridge Casino Hotel
Indiana Ave. at Boardwalk
Telephone: 609-340-3400
Toll-free reservation: 1-800-257-8585
Room rates: Weekdays $90-$100; weekends $110-$120
Summer: Weekdays $110-$120; weekends $130-$140

Recreational facilities: Game room, glass enclosed pool, steam and
sauana rooms, exercise equipment, suntan salon and whirlpools.
664-seat Palace Theater

Table games: 77 tables including 53 blackjack, 12 craps

Slot machines: 1,239 machines: 75 5-cent, 866 25-cent, 110 50-
cent, 188 $1

Harrah's Marina Hotel Casino
1725 Brigantine Blvd.
Telephone: 609-441-5000
Toll-free reservation: 1-800-242-7724

Room rates:	Sept. 16–Nov. 15, 1988		Nov. 16-Mar. 31, 1989	
	Weekday	Weekend	Weekday	Weekend
Atrium Tower	$115	$135	$105	$125
Double or King	$95	$115	$85	$105
	Apr. 1–Jun. 14, 1989		June. 15–Sept. 15, 1989	
Atrium Tower	$115	$135	$140	$155
Double or King	$95	$115	$120	$135

Recreational facilities: Swimming pool, exercise room, fun center
for children and teenagers plus 850-seat theater

Table games: 100 tables

Slot machines: 1,700 slot machines

Resorts International Casino-Hotel
Boardwalk and North Carolina Ave.
Telephone: 609-344-6000
Toll-free reservation: 1-800-GET-RICH
Room rates: North Tower Mid Week–$65 + 12% tax
North Tower Weekends–$95 + 12% tax
East Tower Mid Week–$90-$150 + 12% tax
East Tower Weekends–$125-$160 + 12% tax

Recreational facilities: Whirlpool, steam room, workout room and
game room

Table games: 117 tables including 78 blackjack, 20 craps

Slot machines: 1,672 machines

Sands Hotel, Casino and Country Club
Indiana Ave. and Brighton Park
Telephone: 609-441-4000
Toll-free reservation: 1-800-257-8580

Room rates: Nov. 29, 1988 - Mar. 26, 1989
        Sunday thru Thursday $99-$119
        Friday, Saturday and holidays–$119-$139
        Plaza Club $129-$149
Recreational facilities: 18-hole golf course, health club features in-
    door-outdoor pool, jacuzzi, Nautilus fitness center, sauna, tan-
    ning booths plus 850-seat Copa Room
Table games: 94 tables including 57 blackjack, 21 craps
Slot machines: 1,449 machines: 76 5-cent, 1,048 25-cent, 111 50-
    cent, 214 $1

Showboat Hotel-Casino
801 Boardwalk
Telephone: 609-343-4000
Toll-free reservation: 1-800-621-0200
Room rates: Winter: Mid Week $85-$95; Weekends $125
        Summer: Mid Week $115; Weekends $160 (July 1-
        Sept. 17)
Recreational facilities: 60-lane bowling center, outdoor pool, minia-
    ture golf course plus 1400-seat Mississippi Pavilion for super
    stars. 350-seat Mardi Gras lounge
Table games: 74 blackjack, 22 craps
Slot machines: 1,600 machines

TropWorld Casino and Entertainment Resort
Brighton and Boardwalk
Telephone: 609-340-4000
Toll-free reservation: 1-800-257-6227

Room rates:	Mid Week (Sun.-Thurs.)	Weekends (Fri.-Sat.)
January	$90	$115
Feb.-Mar.	$95	$125
Apr.,May,June	$115	$135
July-August	$150	$175
Sept.,Oct.,Nov.	$115	$135
December	$90	$115

Recreational facilities: Indoor health clubs with spa, tanning rooms,
    massage area, sauana, exercise room, communal lounge, glass en-
    closed indoor pool, two tennis courts plus 1,700-seat theater
Table games: 147 tables including 110 blackjack, 20 craps

Slot machines: 2,368 machines: 119 5-cent, 1,301 25-cent, 334 50-cent, 591 $1, 23 $5

Trump Castle Hotel & Casino
Huron Ave. & Brigantine Blvd.
Telephone: 609-441-2000
Room rates: Weekdays $75-$135; Weekends $95-$135
Recreational facilities: Health club
Table games: 117 tables including 74 blackjack, 24 craps
Slot machines: 1,684 machines: 86 5-cent, 1,051 25-cent, 319 50-cent, 228 $1

Trump Plaza Hotel and Casino
Boardwalk at Mississippi Ave.
Telephone: 609-441-6000
Toll-free reservation: 1-800-523-2803
Room rates: Weekdays $120; weekends $130
Summer: Weekdays $120; Weekends $140
Recreational facilities: Indoor pool, 2 outdoor tennis courts, shuffle-board, weight room, saunas, video arcade plus a 750-seat theater
Table games: 115 tables including 80 blackjack, 20 craps
Slot machines: 1,173 machines: 96 5-cent, 1,004 25-cent, 257 50-cent, 301 $1, 15 $5

Trump Taj Mahal Casino Resort
1000 Boardwalk, P.O. Box 208
Telephone: 609-449-1000
Toll-free reservations: 1-800-TAJ-TRUMP
Room rates: weekdays $120; weekends $140
Recreational facilities: Indoor Olympic pool, beach and bathing facilities, saunas, 12 restaurants, etc.
Table games: 160 tables including craps, "21," roulette, wheel of fortune, etc.
Slot machines: 3,000

CHAPTER 18

Blackjack in Nevada

Before Atlantic City's Resorts International opened its doors for the eager gambler back in 1978, the only action to be found in the United States was in Nevada. Gambling was legalized there in 1931 and soon it became the gaming capital of the world. This distinction lasted until 1986 when Atlantic City pulled even and subsequently took the lead. Be that as it may, Nevada will always (barring some nuclear disaster) be one of the world's great gaming centers. Here, unlike Atlantic City, every casino makes its own rules, so the games have infinite variety. And the casinos have infinite variety. They range from a complete resort, a self-contained suburb like the MGM Grand Hotel in Las Vegas to the smallest hole-in-the-wall offering but a few tables.

To digress for a moment from the serious business of blackjack to dwell on the good life, here is a thumbnail sketch of what you will find at the MGM Grand Hotel's resort complex spread over forty-three acres:

- A huge gaming casino
- A shopping arcade
- Seven restaurants
- Two nightclubs with big-name stars
- A movie theater which shows classic movies
- A jai alai fronton
- Ten night-lighted tennis courts
- Two swimming pools

- A therapy pool that can hold fifty normal-sized people
- Golf privileges at a nearby country club
- 2,900 guest rooms with a metal star on every door. The management considers every guest a star. And some of these rooms have mirrored ceilings. You don't have to be a sex pervert to enjoy this kind of luxury.
- The Cafe Gigi has ornate gold wall panels and mirrors and an eye-catching door from the movie set of *Marie Antoinette* .

You could spend an entire vacation here without venturing out. Even if you lose at the blackjack tables, your visit here will be worth remembering.

When we speak of Nevada gambling, we're talking about two areas and two sets of rules: the Las Vegas variety and the rules of North Nevada which includes Reno, Stateline, Sparks, Verdi and Carson City. Generally speaking, the Vegas rules are kinder to the bettor than those in the Reno/Tahoe area. So, we'll begin by looking at the Vegas game.

Vegas, too, can be divided into two areas: downtown Las Vegas and "The Strip," a 3 1/2 mile boulevard just south of the city limits. In both areas, you will encounter a great variety of rules and play either 1-, 2-, 4-, 5- or 6-deck games. The 1- or 2-deck games will be hand dealt; more than two decks will employ a shoe.

Also, the mechanics of play differ considerably from Atlantic City, where all the players' cards are dealt face-up and you mustn't touch. In Vegas, the players' first two cards are dealt face-down so you must touch. The dealer takes one card face-up, one face-down. Now, if you wish to stand, place your bet over your cards. If you wish to hit, make a gesture indicating you want a hit. If you are unlucky enough to break, turn your cards up to be verified by the dealer who then relieves you of your chips. When you want to split a pair, turn your cards face-up. You also turn your cards face-up if you wish to double-down. You have blackjack! Turn your cards face-up and be paid 3-2.

Question: How do you count cards that are dealt face-down? Answer: It's a bit difficult but good counters overcome all. Here is the sequence: First count the dealer's up-card, then your own two cards. Next, count the cards dealt face-up to the other players. Then, count the cards of the players who break as they turn them over. If a player splits a pair or doubles-down, count the two cards that he shows. Finally, count the dealer's hole card as he turns it over along with any cards that he draws. So there you are card counter. Go for it!

Now for some basic strategy. Since the 1-deck game is more favorable than the multi-deck shoe game, here is the way to play it in Vegas:

Your Hand	Dealer's Up-Card
8	Double on 5 or 6. Otherwise hit.
9	Double on 2 through 6. Otherwise hit.
10	Double on 2 through 9. Otherwise hit.
11	Always double.
12	Stand on 4 through 6. Otherwise hit.
13 through 16	Stand on 2 through 6. Otherwise hit.
17 through 21	Always stand.
A,2 through A,5	Double on 4 through 6. Otherwise hit.
A,6	Double on 2 through 6. Otherwise hit.
A,7	Double on 3 through 6. Stand on 2,7,8. Hit on 9, 10, or A.
A,8	Double on 6. Otherwise stand.
A,9	Always stand.
A,A	Always split.
2,2	Split on 3 through 7. Otherwise hit.
3,3	Split on 4 through 7. Otherwise hit.
4,4	Double on 5 or 6. Otherwise hit.
5,5	Double on 2 through 9. Otherwise hit.
6,6	Split on 2 through 6. Otherwise hit.
7,7	Split on 2 through 7. Otherwise hit.
8,8	Always split.
9,9	Split on 2 through 9, exc. 7. Stand on 7, 10, A.
10,10	Always stand.

Owing to the difference in rules, basic strategy for the 1-

deck games in the Reno/Tahoe area is slightly different. Here are the differences:

Your Hand	Dealer's Up-Card
8	Always hit.
9	Always hit.
A,2 through A,6	Always hit.
A,7	Stand on 2 through 8. Otherwise hit.
A,8 and A,9	Always stand.
4,4	Always hit.

The multi-deck basic strategy is the same as Atlantic City. As far as hitting goes, this is what you do:

HITTING HARD HANDS

Hit Until You Reach	Dealer's Up-Card
Hard 13	2 or 3
Hard 12	4 through 6
Hard 17	7 through A

HITTING SOFT HANDS

Hit Until You Reach	Dealer's Up-Card
Soft 19	9, 10 or A
Soft 18	Everything else

Never stand on a soft 17

Conventional surrender (surrendering after the dealer checks for blackjack) is permitted in some Nevada casinos. This means you give up your hand and lose one-half your bet, which is better than losing your entire bet if you are stuck with a poor hand against a dealer's strong up-card. Always surrender the following hands:

Your Hand	Dealer's Up-Card
15	10 or Ace
16	9, 10 or Ace

Insurance is available in all Nevada casinos and for a good

reason: The odds favor the house. So never, never take insurance.

Part of the fun of playing blackjack in Nevada is looking for the best games. If you are a very conservative bettor, downtown Las Vegas may be attractive since the minimum betting range may be as low as $2. It is not likely, however, that you'll find head-to-head play with a dealer at a low-minimum table. If you are looking for action, head-to-head play is highly desirable since a fast dealer can give you about 200 games an hour. At a full table, you'll be lucky to play seventy games. Another disadvantage of a full table is that in a 1-deck game, you will be dealt only two hands before a shuffle which means that card counting is out. Among the things to look for while seeking a good game are the surrender rule, liberal doubling-down and splitting, and being permitted to resplit and double-down after splitting pairs.

Some of the best games in downtown Las Vegas are at the El Cortez and the Fremont. On "The Strip," you should check out Caesars Palace, Circus Circus and the MGM.

A caveat: Nevada casinos change their rules quite often, so any list of good games may be out-of-date. But at least the casinos mentioned above are worth a visit.

CHAPTER 19

Blackjack in the Caribbean

The Bahamas

Although the Bahamas, strictly speaking, are not in the Caribbean (everyone knows they are in the Atlantic Ocean about fifty miles off the coast of Florida), they come close enough geographically and in blackjack rules to include in the Caribbean group.

There are five casinos operating in the Bahamas. Three are located on New Providence Island.

- The Cable Beach Casino—a laid back, casual dress kind of place.
- Merv Griffin's Paradise Island Resort and Casino.
- The new, luxurious Crystal Palace hotel.

The other two are on Grand Bahama:

- Princess Casino formerly called the El Casino. This casino is as opulent as they come.
- Genting Lucayon Beach Hotel's Monte Carlo Casino, which opened in the summer of 1986. The Genting Berhad outfit is one of the largest corporations in Malaysia with large holdings in Australia and the Far East.

All the games are 4-deck shoe games and generally speaking are not as good as those offered at Northern Nevada. You can double-down on 9, 10 or 11 but can't double-down after splitting at the Princess Casino. The dealer stands on a soft 17 and any pair may be split and resplit. A soft 13 through 17 should always be hit. On a soft 18, stand on 2 through 8 and hit on a 9, 10 or Ace. Hit hard hands the same as you do in Nevada:

Hit Until You Reach	Dealer's Up-Card
Hard 13	2 or 3
Hard 12	4 through 6
Hard 17	7 through A

Splitting Pairs	Dealer's Up-Card
2,2	4 through 7
3,3	4 through 7
6,6	3 through 6
7,7	2 through 7
9,9	2 through 9 except 7
8,8	Always
A,A	Always

Doubling-Down	Dealer's Up-Card
11	2 through 10
10	2 through 9
9	3 through 6

Those of you who are familiar with play at Atlantic City and Nevada will notice two differences in the mechanics of play here—neither to the advantage of the bettor. First, the dealers shuffle immediately when the cut card is reached instead of finishing the round. Second, on a $5 blackjack, you don't get paid your $2.50 until you get your second blackjack.

Now for the *real* Caribbean. If you live in the frozen North, the Caribbean is a nice place to spend a winter vacation. If you are a serious blackjack player, you will find the blackjack rules here varying from fair to very poor. Among the more favorable spots are the Dominican Republic, Curacao and St. Martin. Some of the worst games are found in Puerto Rico and Aruba. The other spots are pretty much a mixed bag.

Anyway, listed below in alphabetical order are enough casinos to keep you busy for a long time.

Antigua

There are four casinos on Antigua. The largest and newest is the King's Casino, open seven nights a week for blackjack, craps, roulette and slots.

Aruba

Aruba boasts five casinos all located in the Big Five hotels along Palm Beach: The Americana, the Aruba-Caribbean, the Aruba-Sheraton, the Concorde and the Holiday Inn. The less-than-generous rules feature 5-deck games with doubling-down after splitting, but no resplitting of pairs. The dealer has no hole card and hits on a soft 17. Doubled bets are lost to a dealer's natural. At the Holiday Inn they permit surrender. Shoe basic strategy should be used with the following exceptions:

Hit 11.   Do not double-down on a 10 or Ace.
Hit 8,8.   Do not split on a 10 or an Ace.
Hit A,A.   Do not split on an Ace.

These casinos open after lunch and continue all night.

Colombia

In Cartagena, there is the Casino del Caribe which has one room for table games and another for slots. In Santa Marta, you will find the Puerto Galeon which is a replica of a Spanish galleon. In San Andrean, there are casinos at the Royal Abacoa Hotel and at the Eldorado Hotel. In Medellin, you can play blackjack at the Nutibara Hotel. If you are a conservative bettor you will enjoy playing in Colombia since all the casinos have a low minimum betting range. However, the casinos are open only six hours a night—between 9:00 P.M. and 3:00 A.M.

Curacao

There are four casinos in Curacao all using the 4-deck game:

- Princess Isle Hotel. You may double-down on 8 through 11. However, they deal about one-half of a 4-deck shoe, so forget counting.
- Holiday Beach Hotel. They burn five cards and do not permit resplitting of pairs, but your split bet is returned if the dealer has blackjack. Double-down is permitted on 10 and 11 only.
- Plaza. Burns one card and shows it. Otherwise the rules are the same as the Holiday Beach Hotel.
- Hilton. You will find the same rules as the Holiday Beach Hotel and the Plaza.

Dominican Republic

Five casinos operate on this island and they all offer (as far as the Caribbean is concerned) worthwhile games. One of the best is Waldo's at the Jaragua Hotel. Here you can double-down on any number and double-down after splitting pairs.

The others are:

- Neon 2002 at the Hispaniola Hotel.
- NACO. This casino offers good rules including surrender.
- The El Embajador where they burn four cards. Most players find it hard to make a buck here.
- Maunaloa at the Centro de los Heros.

The minimum bet in all these casinos is $5.

Haiti

On Haiti, you will find Mike McLaney's International Casino on Harry Truman Boulevard. This is a small casino with only four blackjack tables. It attracts a lot of gamblers during the winter season and when a cruise ship pulls in. Another McLaney establishment is at the Royal Haitian Hotel and Casino, located on a sixteen-acre estate on the road heading out of town toward Habitation Leclerc.

Martinique

There are only two casinos on this volcanic island: Meridien and La Bateliere. Both are rather plush and charge admission fees. In addition, to gain entrance, you must produce your passport or driver's license.

Puerto Rico

You will find a number of casinos on Puerto Rico mostly in the San Juan-Condado area. They are controlled by the government for operation and granting of licences. Most of them open their doors at 1:00 P.M. and remain open until 4:00 A.M. Some are rather formal, requiring a jacket and tie, but this custom is slowly eroding. Play at the El San Juan Hotel is very slow because you cash your chips at the table instead of taking them to the cashier. The rules in Puerto Rico are among the worst in the Caribbean. In the 4-deck game, the cut card is placed at least one deck from the rear of the shoe. Doubling-down is permitted after splitting, but no resplits are allowed. However, split aces can draw more than one card. The minimum bet at all casinos is $5.

St. Kitts

Yes, Virginia, there is such a place. You will find only one casino on this little island, The Royal St. Kitts.

St. Martin

There are five casinos on this French-Dutch island: Mullet Bay, Great Bay, Little Bay, Concord and Treasure Island Hotel and Casino. The casinos here are smaller and less hyped than those in Puerto Rico and the Bahamas. The blackjack rules at these casinos are as good as any in the Caribbean and the atmosphere is low-key.

St. Vincent

There is but a solitary casino here. The Valley Inn.

CHAPTER 20

Blackjack in Europe

You will find a blackjack game in progress almost anywhere in Europe. As far as the rules are concerned, go to France. The worst are found in Spain, Portugal and Austria.

France

There are about 150 casinos in France, all with beatable rules. The best of the lot is Loews Monte Carlo which offers the most favorable rules of any casino in Europe. The only bad feature—and this rule is true in all of Europe: the dealer does not take his hole card until all the players have played their hands. And, come to think of it, what's so bad about that? But most of the blackjack pros say it's bad and we'll have to let it go at that. Like most of Europe and the Caribbean, Loews employs a 4-deck game and follows Las Vegas rules. It has, in fact, a strong Las Vegas flavor and is more like an American casino than a European one featuring Bally slot machines, American-type roulette and the Big Six wheel. The rules say you can split any pair and double-down on split pairs. The cut card placement is about 1-deck from the rear of the shoe.

By contrast, the world-famous Big Casino at Monte Carlo is completely European and the rules are not quite as good as Loews Monte Carlo. For example, six decks are used with the cut card placed from 1- to 1½-decks from the rear of the shoe. You can double-down on 9, 10 and 11, split and resplit pairs and double-down on split pairs. Not surprisingly, there are no low-minimum bets at this casino, so bring money. Blackjack games begin in late afternoon in two rooms: the "Salons Ordinaires" for the great unwashed where playing stops at 1:00 A.M., and the "Salons Prives" which stays open as long as the action continues. Both rooms charge admission fees: a small one for "Salons Ordinaires" and a higher one for "Salons Prives."

For once, forget whether blackjack rules are good or bad; the Big Casino has to be recommended. It is truly unique and unlike any U.S. casino in that it has clocks and windows. The ambiance is grand-scale. The croupiers wear tuxedoes and the waiters, white uniforms. If you are a people watcher (and who isn't?), you will enjoy following the play of formally attired gentlemen and their well-coiffed ladies. So, whether you decide to play or not, if you are in the area, it is well worth a visit.

For the remaining 100-plus casinos in France, the rules vary in each. Some allow doubling-down on 9, 10 and 11, splitting any pair and identical 10's. But they all have these rules in common:

4 to 6 decks
European no hole card
Stand on soft 17
Insurance
Pay 3-to-2 for blackjack

Several casinos on the French Riviera offer better-than-average games. They include Canet Plage, St. Raphael and Antibes. Scattered throughout France, especially at Biarritz, Dieppe and Nederbraun, are some of the finest casinos in Europe.

Germany

There are quite a few casinos operating in West Germany. Fairly good games may be found in Baden-Baden, Frankfurt and Hamburg. One of the best is at the Spielbank Hamburg atop the Hotel International Hamburg. A 5-deck game is employed there with somewhat liberal rules. You can double-down on 9, 10 and 11 and split any pair. Unlike Atlantic City with its eye-in-the-sky, signaling is not permitted. The player must state his intention. If you do not like the distraction of playing in a large casino, this place is for you. You play in a quiet, club-like atmosphere. There are but two blackjack tables. This casino, like most in Europe, opens its doors at 3:00 P.M.

England

The blackjack rules in England are rather neutral—neither good nor bad. Most casinos observe the following rules:

4-deck games
Double-down on 9, 10 and 11
Double-down on split pairs
No resplitting of pairs
Good cut card placement
Low minimum tables

There is one rule that sets England's casinos apart from the rest of the world. You must be a member to be admitted, but this is done easily enough. Apply for membership wherever you wish to play and forty-eight hours later you become a member in good standing.

This rule is enforced as I found to my dismay. Before going to London, a friend loaned me his membership card to the Sportsmen's Club, so I felt it was unnecessary to apply on my arrival. When my wife and I appeared for dinner and a night at the gaming tables, I presented the membership card and was asked to sign my name. I was not prepared for this and my signature, of course, was not a bit like my friend's which was on file. Consequently, we were barred, and when I started to protest, three security guards appeared to press the point. The moral: if you have a friend's membership card, practice his signature. My friend's card, by the way, was destroyed and no longer is he a member in good standing.

Italy

One of the best casinos in Italy, and even here the rules are not that great, is in San Remo on the Gulf of Genoa. San Remo is a beautiful city famous for its flower market, palm-lined boulevards, gardens and beaches. A cable car leads to Mont Gignone which provides a panorama of the Italian and French Rivieras. In addition, the city has countless hotels and about eighty restaurants. But this is a blackjack book not a travelogue. The rules of San Remo say you can double-down on 9, 10 and 11, split pairs up to three times, but no doubling-down on them. Not very generous, are they? But this is the best you can find in Italy.

There is also blackjack action to be had in Venice. Venice, of course, is one of the world's loveliest cities, but don't go there to play blackjack. The two casinos here are The Municipal on the Grand Canal, open from October to May and charging admission of about $12, and the Lido, open only during the summer season.

Both casinos favor the 2-deck game and permit doubling-down on 11 only. The dealer randomly shuffles the cut card in with the two decks, so you'll be playing approximately one deck. The minimum bet is about $6.

Belgium

Four casinos offer beatable games of blackjack. They are Oostende, Knokkeheist, Blankenberg and Middelkerke. Here are the rules:

    4-deck game
    Double-down on 9, 10 and 11
    Double-down after splits

Dealer stands on soft 17
Pairs cannot be resplit
Cut card is placed about ½-deck from the rear of the shoe.

Holland

Casinos can be found in Zandvoort and Valkenburg. The rules here are fairly good since they are about the same as Belgium, except that the dealers are not as kind. Here the cut card is placed about 1-deck from the rear of the shoe.

Other countries in Europe that feature blackjack are Spain, Portugal and Austria. No casinos are recommended in these countries since the rules are very poor without exception.

CHAPTER 21

Blackjack in the Rest of the World

Good blackjack games may be found in many parts of the world, particularly in Macao and Korea, but for the most part the rules are not nearly as favorable as you will find in the United States. In South America, for example, the rating scale ranges from fair to poor. Some of the better games are played in Argentina where you will have no difficulty in finding a casino. They abound. However, you will have to put in a lot of mileage between casinos since they are not concentrated the way they are in Atlantic City and Nevada. So, for starters, let's take a look at the South American scene.

Argentina

Mar del Plato along the Atlantic coast about 200 miles south of Buenos Aires has three casinos. The largest one has room for 5,000 people to play at one time.

- Just south of Mar del Plato at Necochea there is a casino which boasts that it is the largest in the world. So you can see that when it comes to gambling in the Argentine, the accent is on big.
- There are casinos near Santiago located at Mendoza, San Luis, Alto Gracia and Cordoba.
- In North Central Argentina, casinos can be found at Santiago del Estero, Salta and Tucuman.

• In Southwestern Argentina on Lake Nahuel Huapi, there is a casino in Bariloche.

Chile

The largest casino in Chile is the Municipal Casino in Vina del Mar located just south of the port of Valparaiso on the Pacific. There are also casinos in Puerto Varas and Penuelas. They are open daily in season which runs from September 15 to March 15 and on weekends during the rest of the year.

Paraguay

A recent arrival with very pleasant decor is the casino in the Hotel Ita Enramada. It's quite formal and gentlemen must dress in a jacket and tie. A small admission fee is charged. Another casino, Presidente Stroessner, overlooks the Parana River where the Friendship bridge connects Paraguay with Brazil.

Uruguay

Casino-hotels will be found at Carrasco, Atlantida, Piriapolis and Punta del Este. All these casinos are located along the Atlantic Coast near the capital city of Montevideo.

Egypt

There are three casinos operating in the large hotels in Cairo: The Hilton, Shepheards and the Sheraton. There is one in Alexandria: the Cecil Hotel. If you play in these casinos, you will not rub shoulders with the natives. Egyptians are forbidden to play or even enter the gaming rooms. Here you must show your passport to be admitted.

Australia

At Broadbeach on the Gold Coast, you can play in Jupiters

Casino in the Conrad International Hotel. However, you just don't walk in. The clubs in this country are private, but a phone call will open the doors for you. Just show your passport or drivers license. There are other casinos in Australia, but Jupiters is the "in" casino frequented by many celebrities—or so they say.

Macao

The casino to play on this island just a short distance from Hong Kong is located in the Lisboa Hotel. The rules here are quite good but avoid the 1-deck game since they shuffle after every hand. They offer every good rule in the book including surrender except for doubling-down which is permitted on 11 only. The cut card placement is excellent—often less than 1/2-deck from the rear of the shoe. A caveat: Patience is a must. Chinese are very, very slow players.

Korea

In Seoul, you will find a good game at Walker Hill. The 4-deck game is used and the cut card is placed less than 1/2-deck from the rear of the shoe. However, forget playing for large stakes because you won't be able to get your money out of the country. It's a beatable game but don't be greedy.

Well, that's about it, fellow blackjack players. The world can be viewed as one huge casino. And if you are inclined to be a high-roller, travel expenses and hotel room will be on the house. Big name shows and drinks, too, will be offered as comps. All you have to do is apply for a credit line and play with black chips. If you feel more comfortable with a low betting range, fine. The important thing is to enjoy the game, and you will enjoy it if you play well.

Glossary of Blackjack Terms

ACTION—The total amount of money wagered by a player.

BACK COUNTING—Taking a position in back of the players and counting down the shoe.

BASIC STRATEGY—The most efficient way for a blackjack player to play a hand. A knowledge of when to hit, stand, split or double-down depending upon the player's cards and the dealer's up-card.

BETTING RANGE—The betting spread used by a player. The betting ratio between the lowest bet and the highest bet.

BLACK—A black $100 chip.

BLACKJACK—An ace and any 10-value card received in the first two cards dealt.

BUST—To lose a hand by exceeding the total of "21."

BREAK—The same as "bust."

CHECK—Casino terminology for a chip.

CLUMP—Any group of high cards. A clump may be used to the advantage of the casino by placement behind the cut card so as to be kept out of play; or used to the advantage of the player who spots a clump and follows it through the shuffle.

COLD DECK—A deck of cards unfavorable to the player.

COMP—Free drinks, food or service given by the casino to a player.

COUNT—The running count. An accumulative plus or minus of all the cards played from the shoe.

COUNTER—A card counter who employs a system to determine whether the shoe is favorable or unfavorable for betting purposes.

CUT CARD—A yellow plastic card inserted into the cards to denote the end of the shoe.

DISCARD TRAY—A container to hold cards already played.

DOUBLE-DOWN—An option that permits a player to double his bet and receive one additional card.

DROP—The total amount of cash and markers taken in at a table.

EARLY SURRENDER—The player's option to surrender one-half his original bet if he believes he has a poor chance of winning the hand, before the dealer checks to see if he has blackjack.

EYE-IN-THE-SKY—Casino employees observing play from above the tables.

FIRST BASE—The first player to receive a card from the dealer. The extreme right-hand seat at the blackjack table.

FLAT BET—To bet the same amount on every hand played.

FLOOR PERSON—A casino employee who supervises the dealers and observes play.

GREEN—A green $25 chip.

HEAT—Being more than casually observed by a pit boss or floor person.

HIT—To request an additional card from the dealer.

HEAD-ON—Just you and the dealer playing alone.

HOLE CARD—The face-down card held by the dealer.

HOT DECK—A deck or shoe favorable to the player.

INSURANCE—An option a player can take when the dealer's up-card is an ace. The player may bet one-half his original bet that the dealer has blackjack; if he does, the player is paid 2 to 1; if not, the player loses.

MECHANIC—A skilled but dishonest dealer. One who deals the second card.

MINUS COUNT—A negative running count of the cards played.

NICKLE—A red $5 chip.

PAINT—A picture card or 10.

PAT HAND—A hand with a total of 17 through 21.

PIT BOSS—A casino employee who supervises a group of gaming tables as well as other casino employees (floor people and dealers) in his area.

PLUS COUNT—A positive running count of the cards played.

PUSH—A tie.

QUARTERS—Green $25 chips.

RED—A red $5 chip.

RUNNING COUNT—The cumulative count of the cards already played.

SCAM—An illegal scheme to defraud a casino.

SHOE—A container to hold the unplayed cards.

SLUG—Any group of high cards. The same as "clump."

SOFT HAND—A hand with an ace that can be counted as either 1 or 11.

SPLIT—An option permitting a player to play two hands and make two bets if he receives an identical pair.

STAND—A player's decision not to draw any additional cards.

STIFF HAND—A weak hand. One totaling 12 through 16.

THIRD BASE—The extreme left-hand seat at the table. The last player before the dealer.

TOKE—A token. A tip given to the dealer.

TRUE COUNT—In advanced play, an adjustment of the running count to the number of cards, decks or half-decks remaining to be played.

UP-CARD—The dealer's exposed card.

Bibliography

Archer, John. *The Archer Method of Winning at 21*. Hollywood, CA: Wilshire, 1978.

Braun, Julian H. *How to Play Winning Blackjack*. Chicago: Data House Publishing Co. 1980.

Canfield, Richard Albert. *Blackjack Your Way to Riches*. Scottsdale, AZ: Expertise Publishing Co. 1977.

Chin, S.Y. *Understanding and Winning Casino Blackjack*. New York: Vantage, 1980.

Donatelli, Dante A. *Blackjack—Total Profit Strategy*. Greenburg, PA: Mar Lee Enterprises, 1979.

Epstein, Richard A. *The Theory of Gambling and Statistical Logic*. New York: Academic Press, 1977.

Goodman, Mike. *Your Best Bet*. New York: Ballantine Books, 1977.

Griffin, Peter A. *The Theory of Blackjack*. Las Vegas: Gamblers Book Club, 1981.

Humble, Lance. *Blackjack Gold*. Toronto: International Gaming, 1976. Retitled *Blackjack Super/Gold*, 1979.

Humble, Lance, and Carl Cooper. *The World's Greatest Blackjack Book*. Garden City, NY: Doubleday & Co., 1980.

Ita, Koko. *21 Counting Methods to Beat 21*. Las Vegas: Gambler's Book Club, 1976.

Noir, Jacques. *Casino Holiday*. Berkeley, CA: Oxford Street Press, 1970.

Patterson, Jerry L. *Blackjack's Winning Formula*. NJ: Casino Gaming Specialists, 1980.

Revere, Lawrence. *Playing Blackjack as a Business*. Secaucus, NJ: Lyle Stuart, 1977.

Roberts, Stanley. *Winning Blackjack*. Los Angeles: Scientific Research Services, 1971.

Rouge et Noir, stall. *Winning at Casino Gaming*. Glen Head, NY: Rouge et Noir, 1975.

Scarne, John. *Scarne's Complete Guide to Gambling*. New York: Simon and Schuster, 1961, 1974.

Smith, Harold S. *I Want to Quit Winners*. Englewood Cliffs, NJ: Prentice-Hall, 1961.

Thorp, Edward O.. *Beat the Dealer*. New York: Random House, 1962. Revised edition: New York: Vintage Books, 1966.

Uston, Ken, and Robert Rapoport. *The Big Player*. New York: Holt, Rinehart & Winston, 1977.

Uston, Ken. *Two Books on Blackjack*. Wheaton, MD: Uston Institute of Blackjack, 1979.

Uston, Ken. *Million Dollar Blackjack*. Los Angeles: SRS Enterprises, 1981.

Wilson, Allan N. *The Casino Gambler's Guide*. New York: Harper & Row, 1977.

Wong, Stanford. *Professional Blackjack*. Las Vegas: Gambler's Book Club, 1977. Revised edition: La Jolla, CA: Pi Yee Press, 1980.

Wong, Stanford. *Winning Without Counting*. La Jolla, CA: Pi Yee Press, 1978.